The Dungeon of Drumming

Book 1

David Lawrence

authorHOUSE®

AuthorHouse™
1663 Liberty Drive
Bloomington, IN 47403
www.authorhouse.com
Phone: 833-262-8899

Published by AuthorHouse 03/18/2022

ISBN: 978-1-6655-5410-7 (sc)
ISBN: 978-1-6655-5409-1 (e)

Library of Congress Control Number: 2022904596

The Dungeon of Drumming

Drumming

Book 1

By David Lawrence

To My Loving wife, Candi!

CARPE DIEM
SEIZE THE DAY!

Introduction

Lawrence School of Drumming welcomes everyone to The Dungeon of Drumming! The goal of this book is three fold: first, to provide a comprehensive drum exercise book to enhance everyone's tool box of drumming techniques to prepare them for a successful lifelong venture as a drummer! Second, to provide a comprehensive guide for each student through their first twenty five lessons with Lawrence School of Drumming! Finally, to provide a "Baby Step" technique to make this process as simple as possible so it would not matter if you are 6 or 60 you will have fun, and you will be a successful student and drummer!

    I have been working with students with these techniques for 12 years now so I know the work! All you have to do is work hard on a consistent basis, play from your heart and you will be a successful and competent drummer!

Acknowledgements

I would like to extend a special thanks to Heid Music, Candi Lawrence, James Lawrence, Chris Lawrence, Bill Lawrence, Jim Weinmann, my Mom and Dad, all my past, present and future students and the rest of my family and loved ones.

Contents

Golden Rule of Lawrence:

Do not under any
circumstances stop playing
during any musical performance!!

The Four Rules of Lawrence:

If you cannot play something:

1. Slow down!!

Note: rule 1 will solve 90% of your problems

2. Break apart the beat and work on just the part you are having problems with!
3. Count out the area of difficulty and play it over and over while counting!
4. Call your Teacher or Mentor with any additional questions!

Five Aspects of Practice

1. Stretch
2. Open Jam
   - Warming up
   - Play from the heart
   - No Music
3. Lesson Material
4. Work on Weaknesses
   - Double Bass drumming
   - Left Hand Playing
   - Working on a new Song
5. Open Jam
   - Soloing
   - Play from the heart
   - No Music

Words of Wisdom

Consistency is the key to greatness!

1/8 Note Rock Beats

1/8 NOTE BEATS

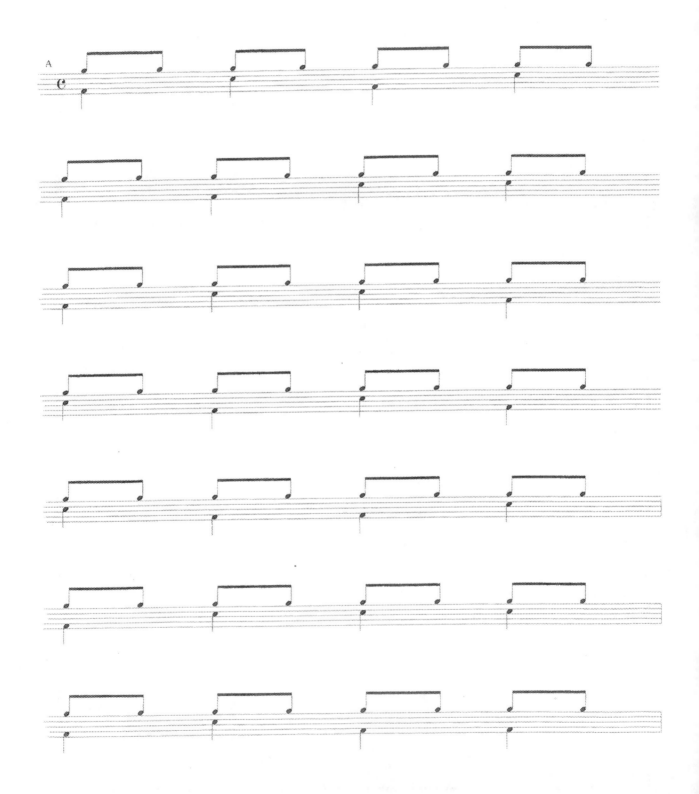

LAWRENCE SCHOOL OF DRUMMING©

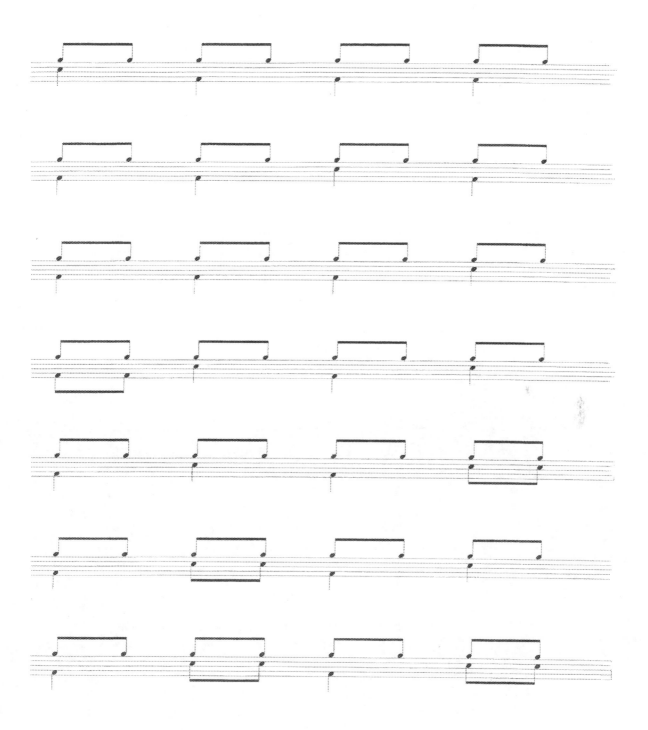

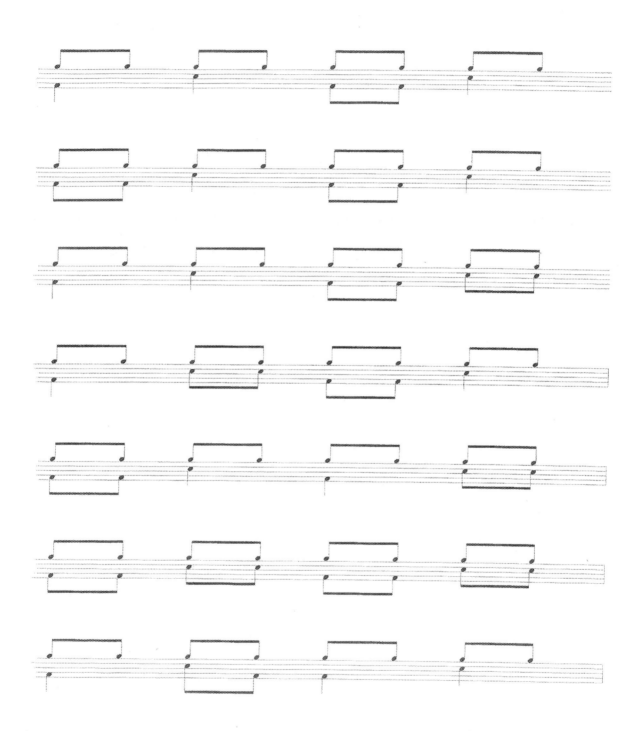

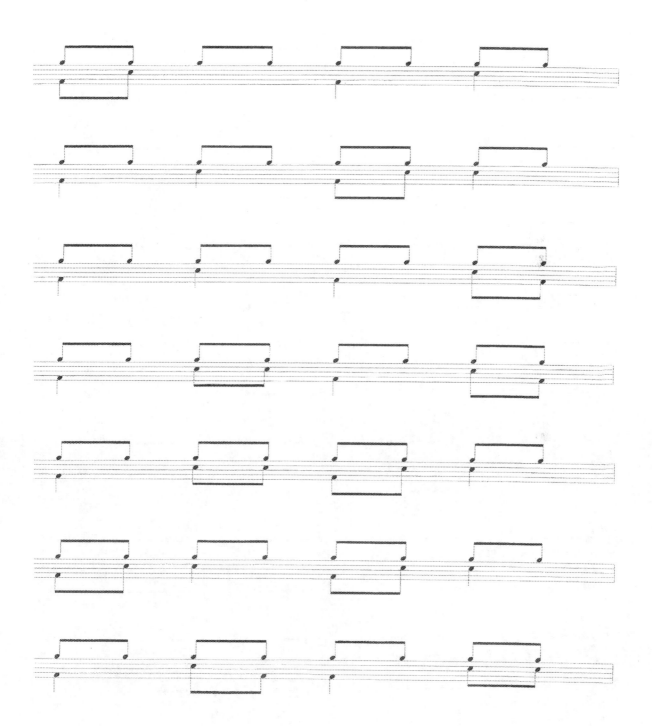

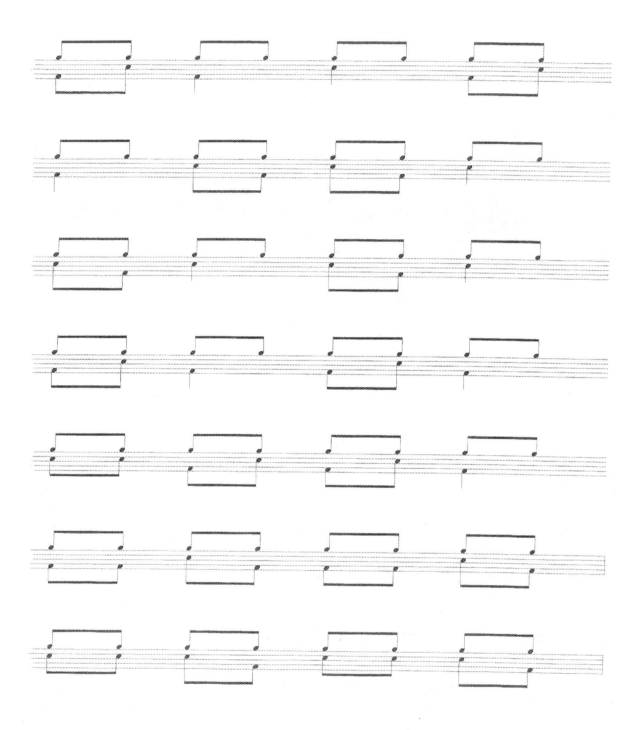

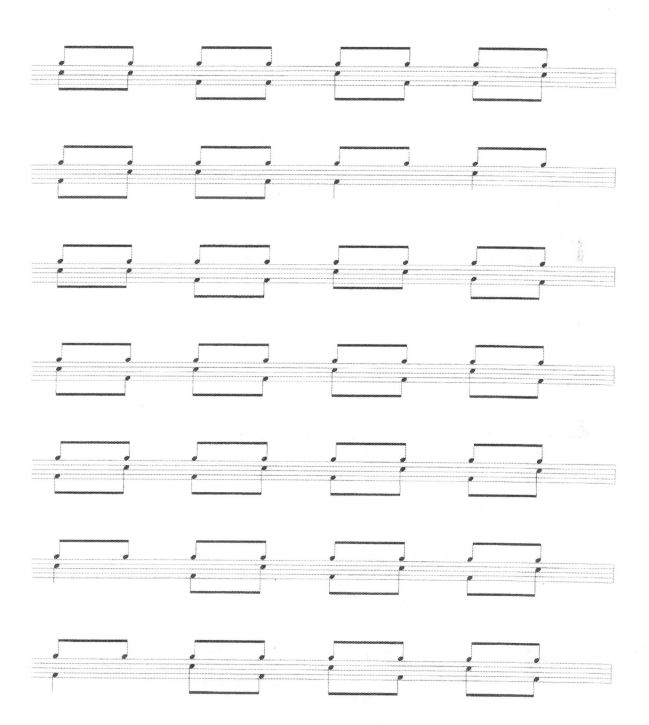

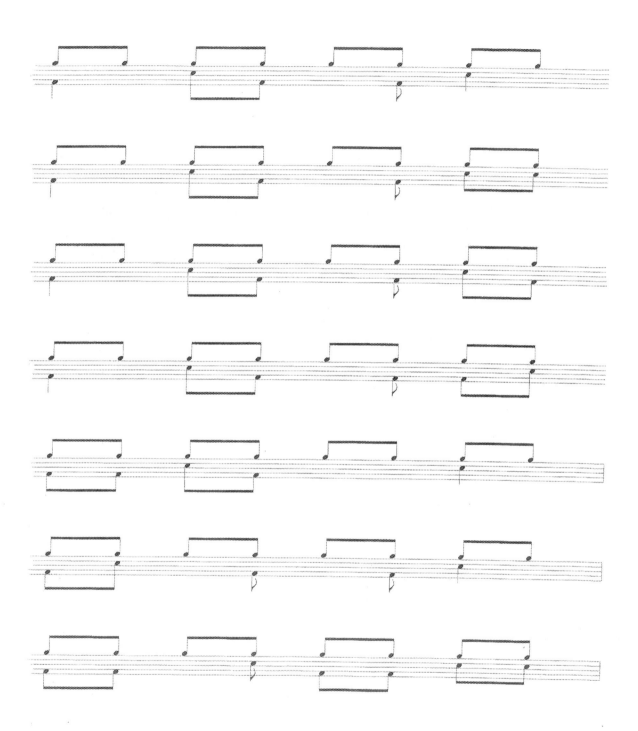

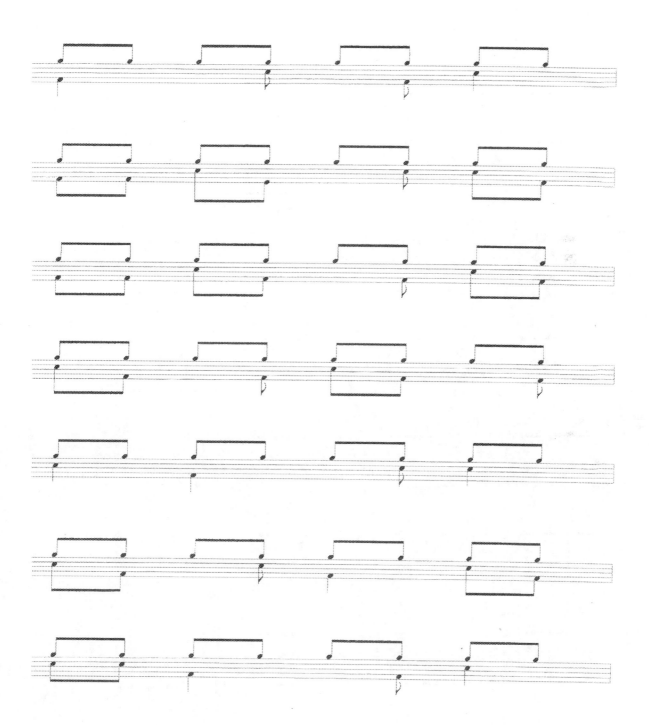

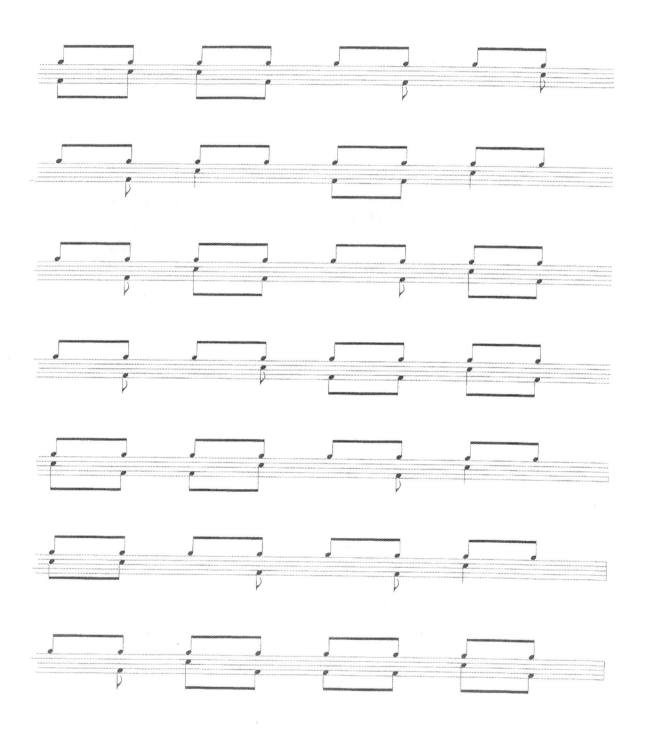

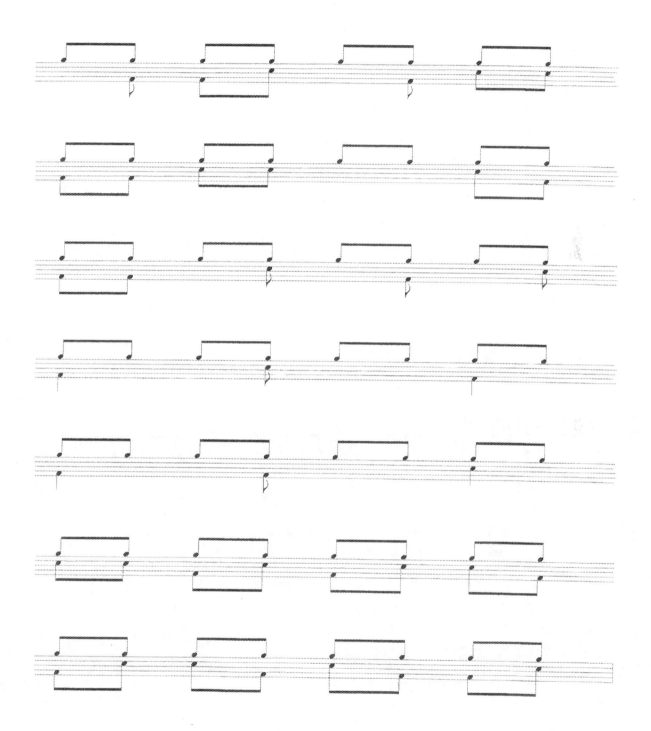

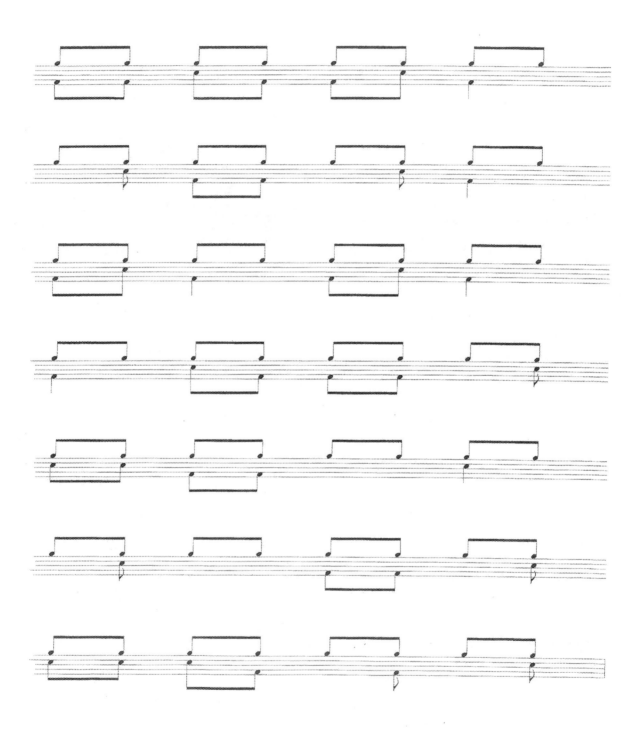

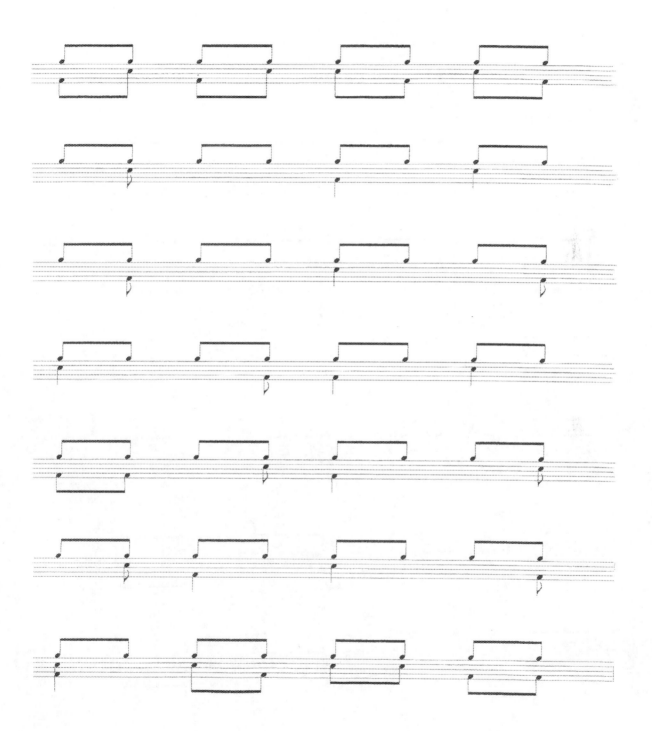

13

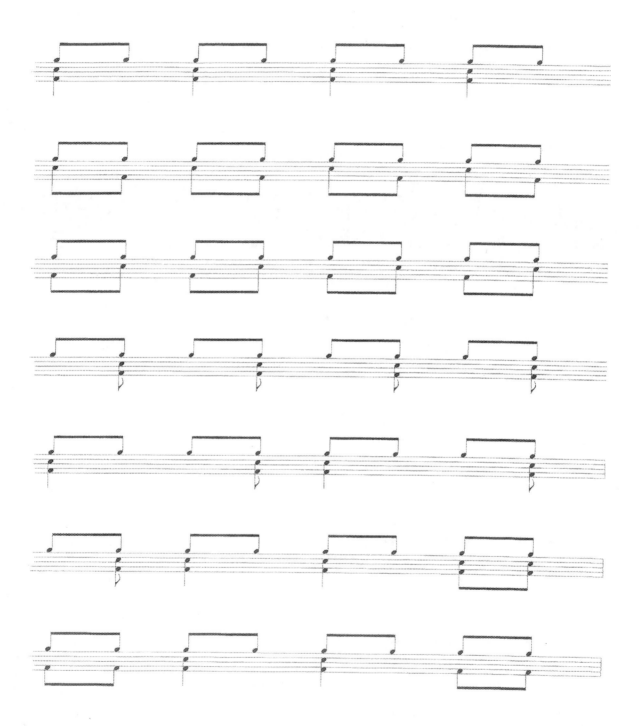

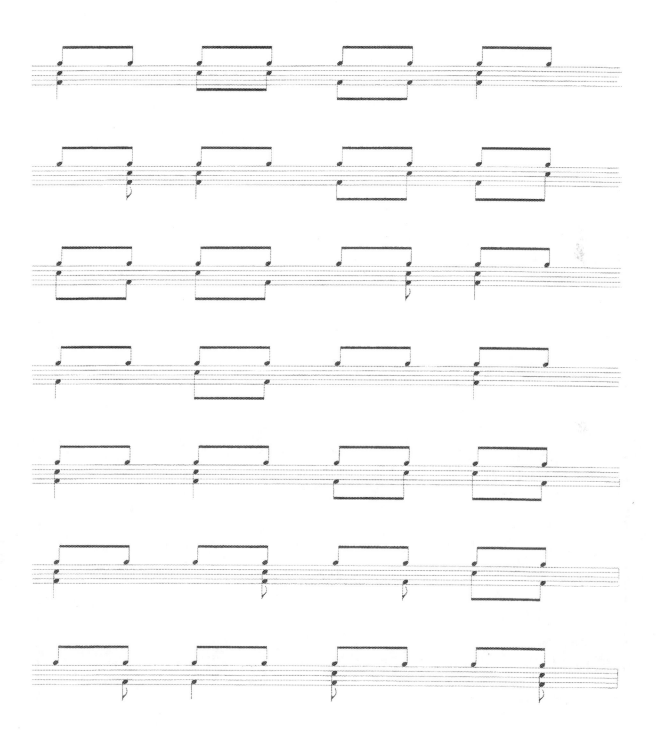

The contrast in life is what makes life so rewarding!

"1 E" Exercises

"1 E" EXERCISES

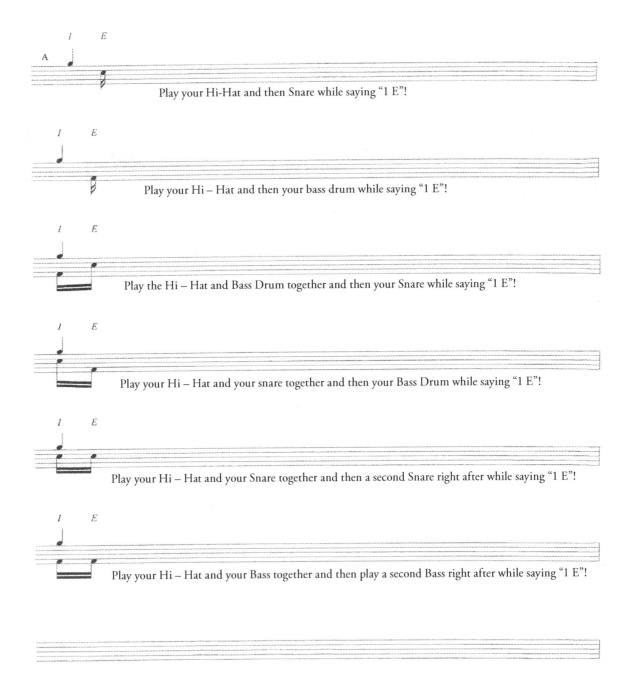

Play your Hi-Hat and then Snare while saying "1 E"!

Play your Hi – Hat and then your bass drum while saying "1 E"!

Play the Hi – Hat and Bass Drum together and then your Snare while saying "1 E"!

Play your Hi – Hat and your snare together and then your Bass Drum while saying "1 E"!

Play your Hi – Hat and your Snare together and then a second Snare right after while saying "1 E"!

Play your Hi – Hat and your Bass together and then play a second Bass right after while saying "1 E"!

Simplicity leads to speed and rememberability!

1/8 Note Syncopated Rock Beats

1/8 NOTE SYNCOPATED BEATS

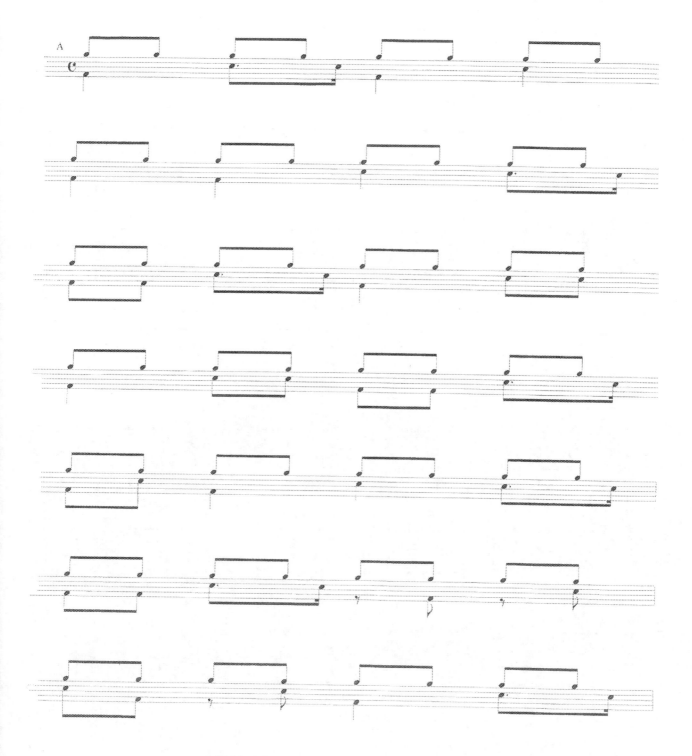

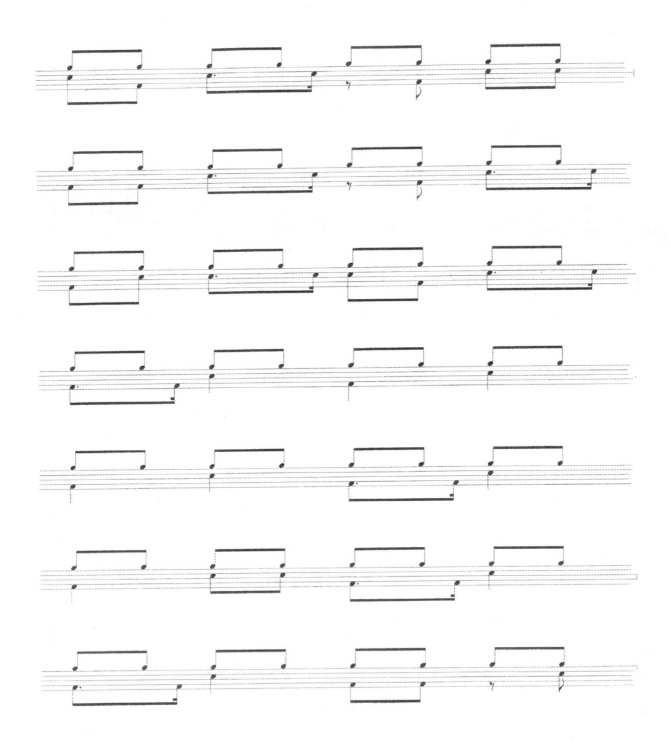

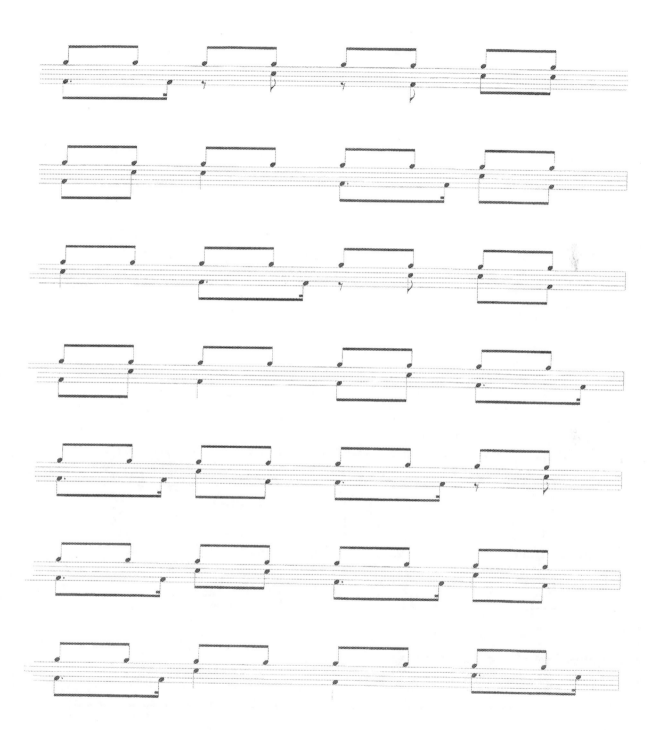

23

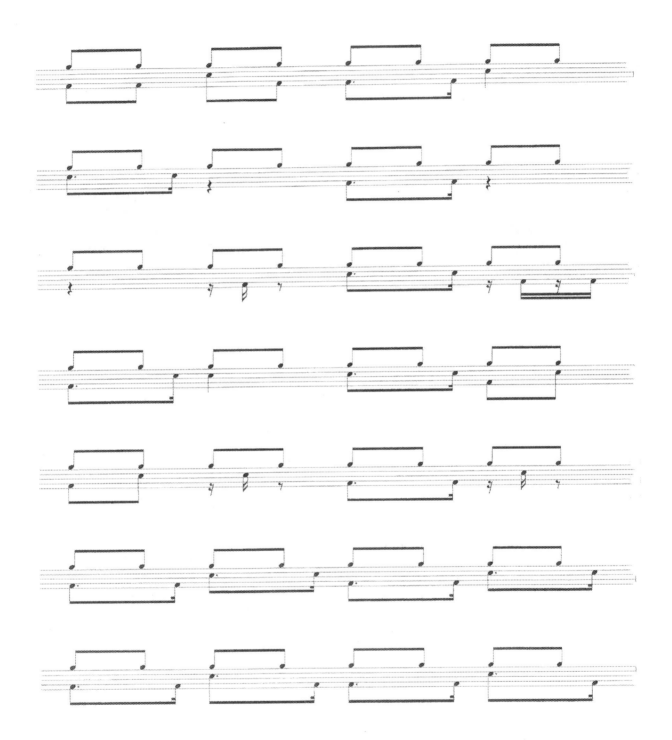

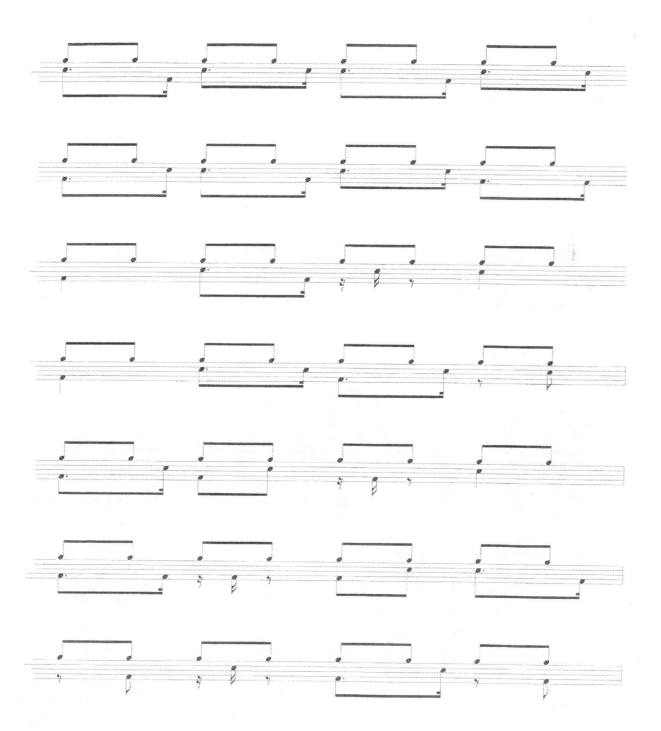

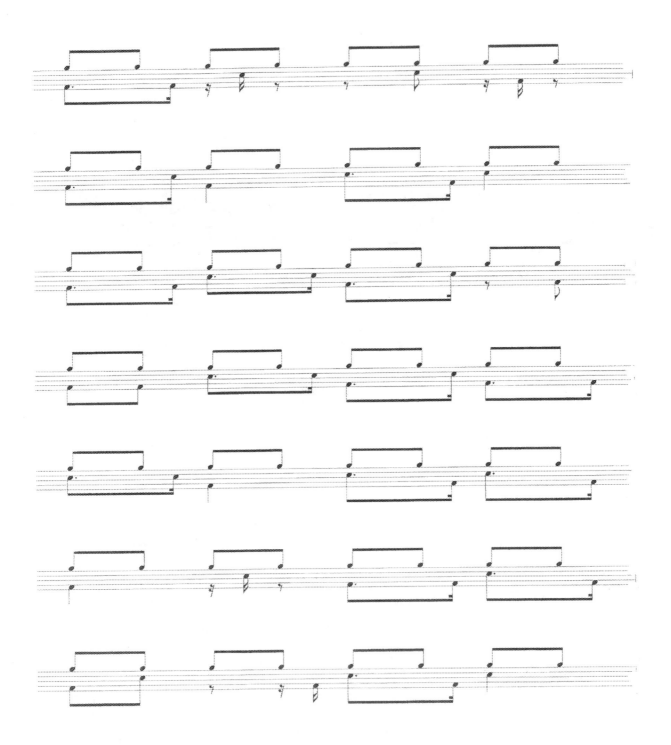

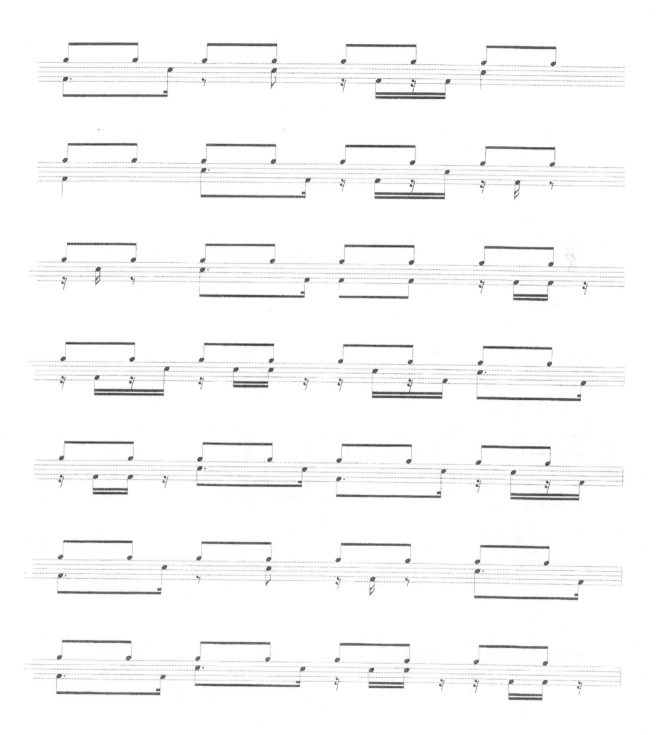

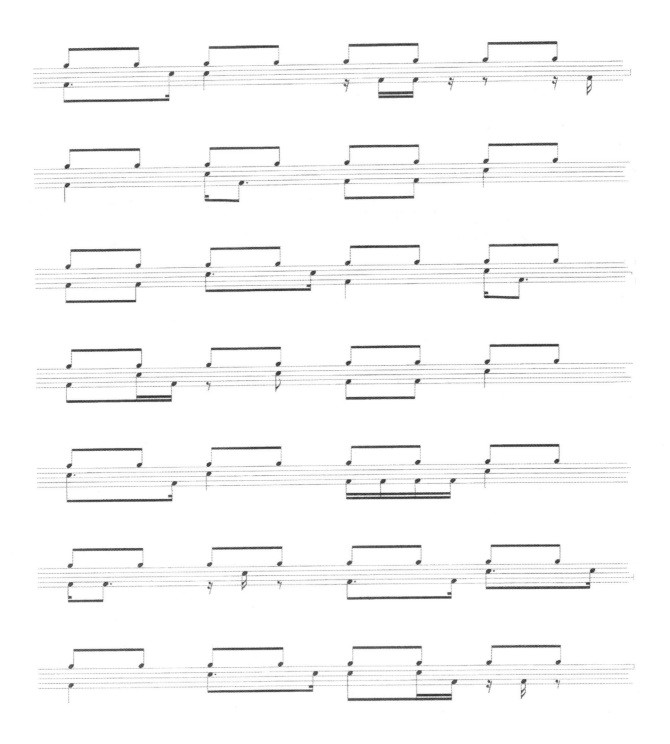

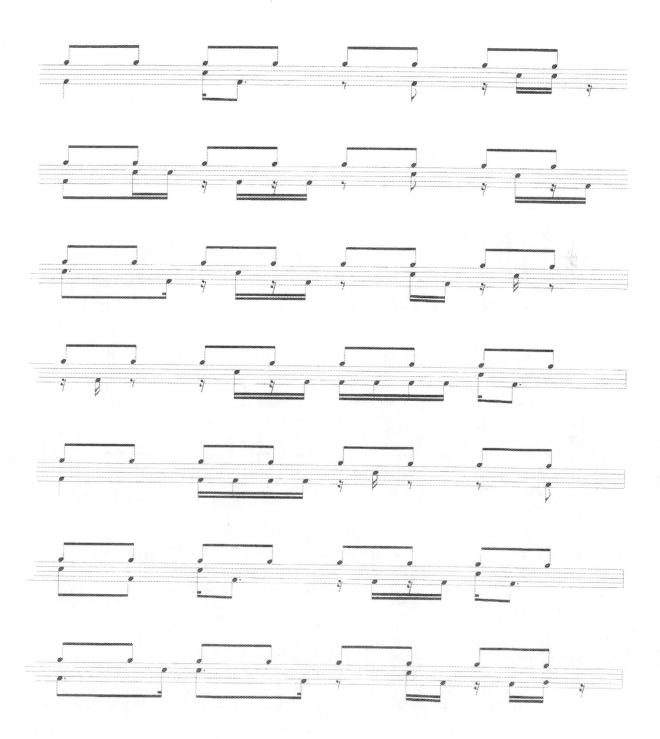

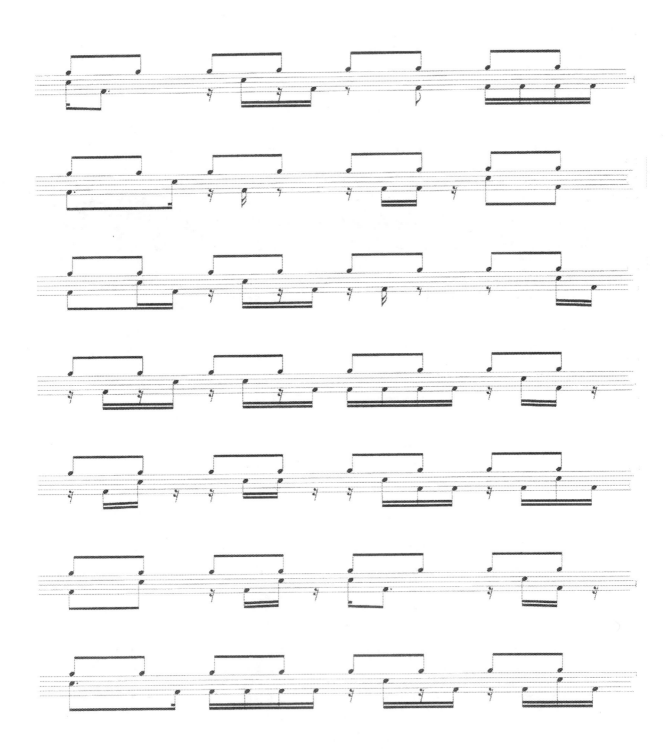

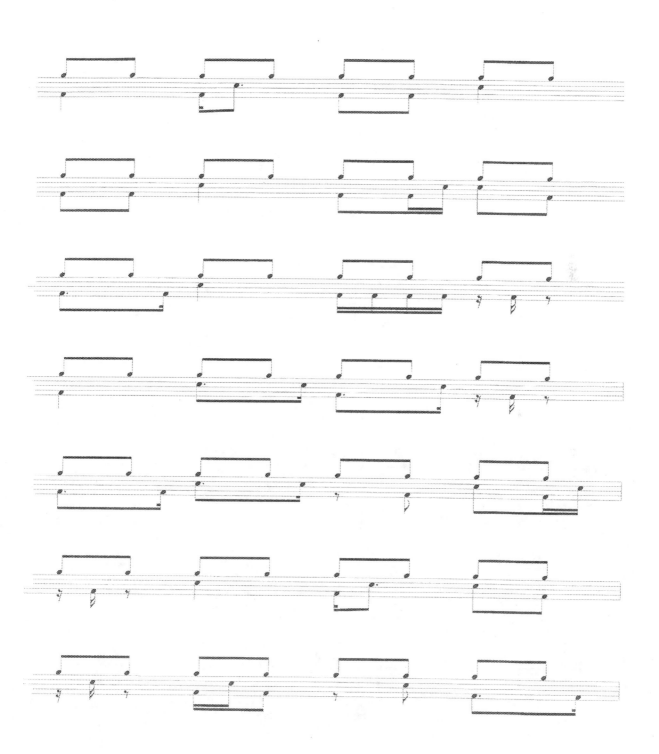

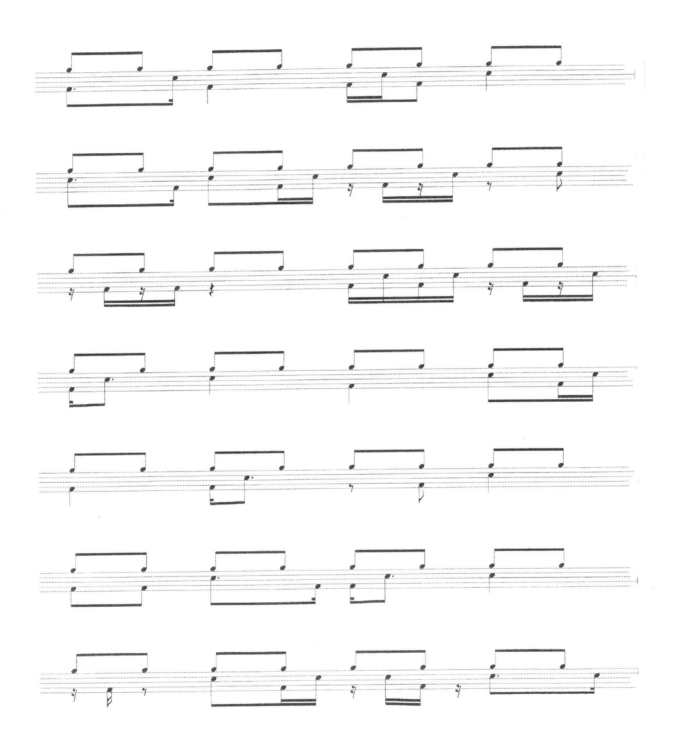

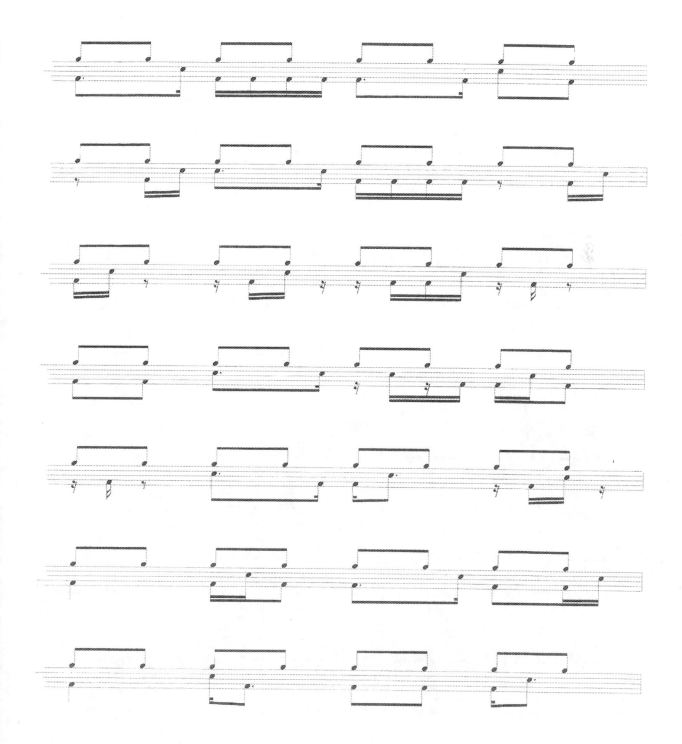

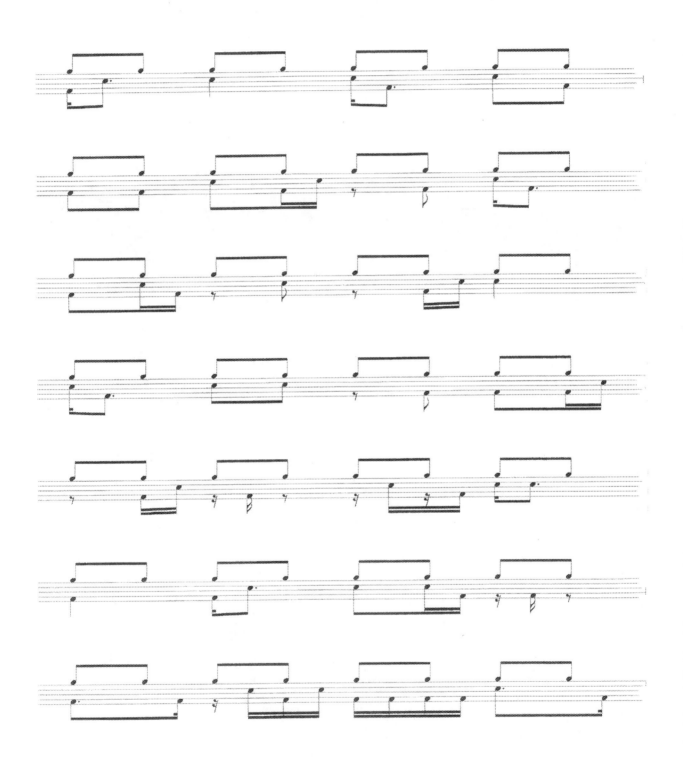

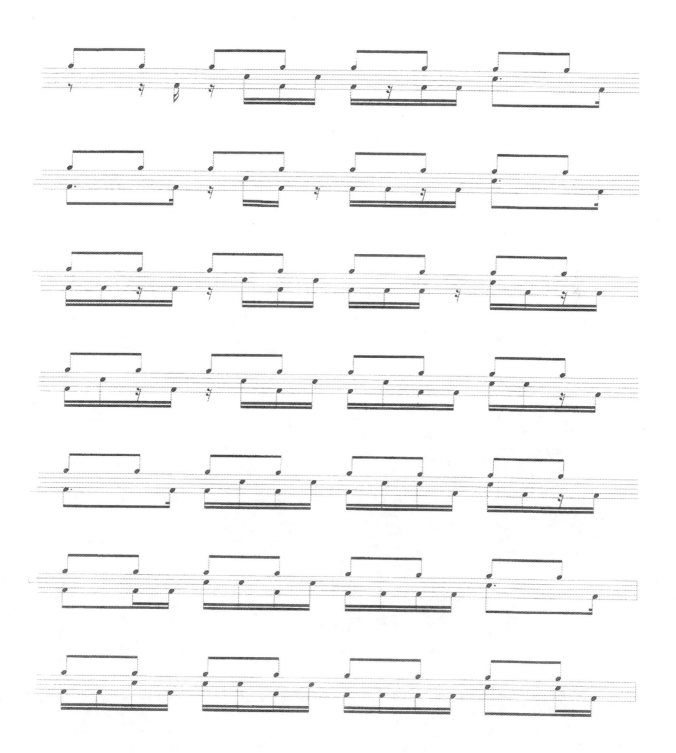

1/8 NOTE SYNCOPATED BEATS
PART 2

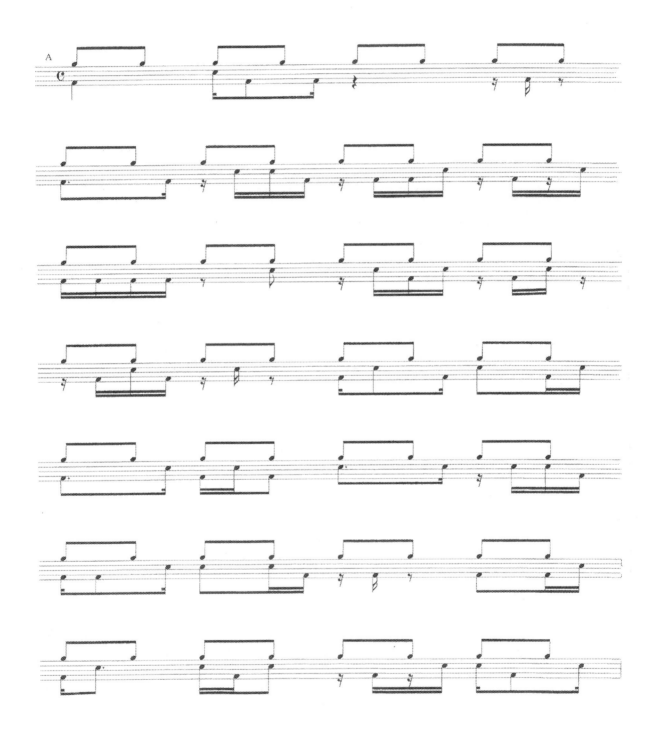

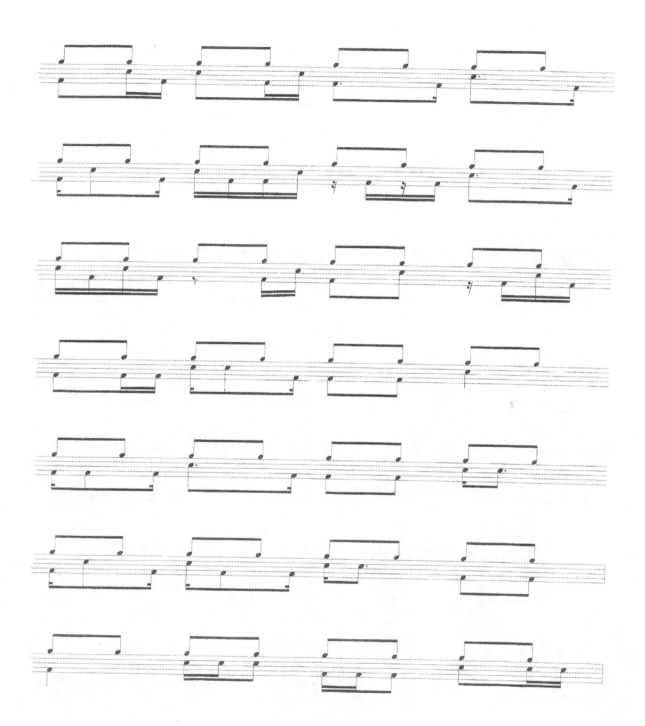

37

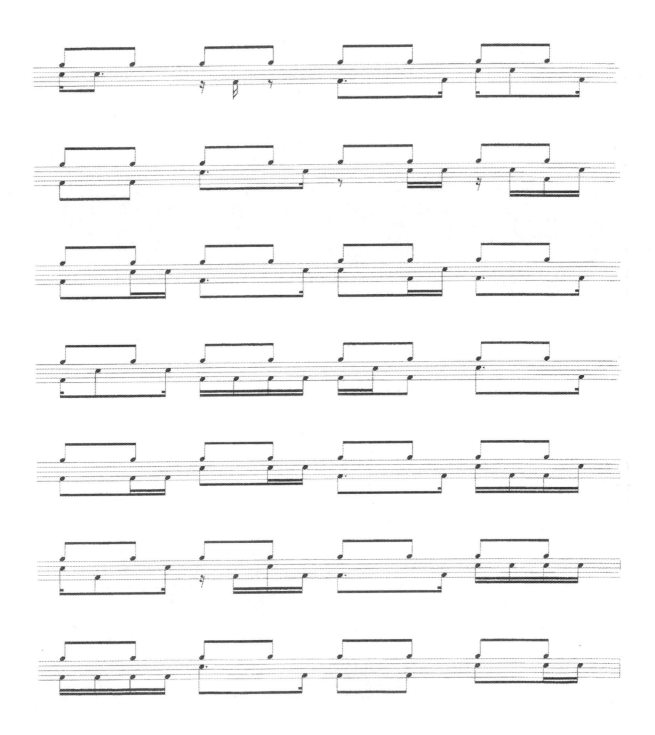

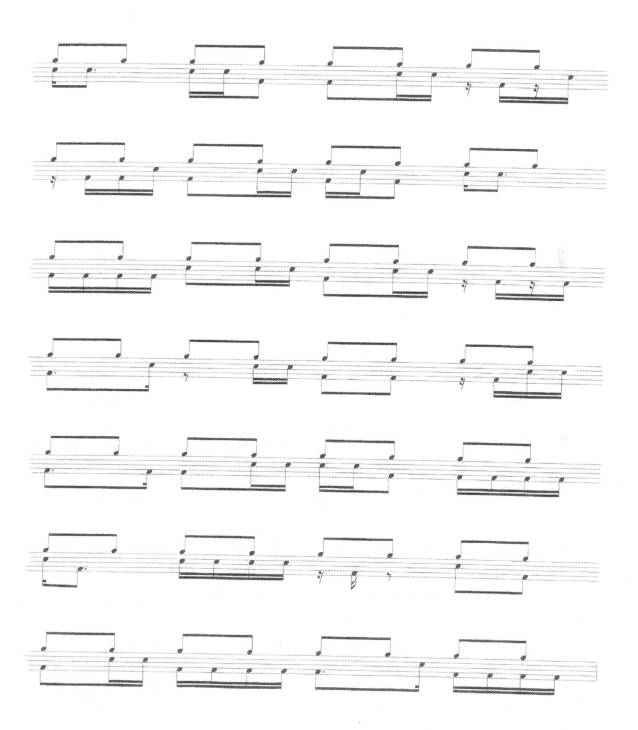

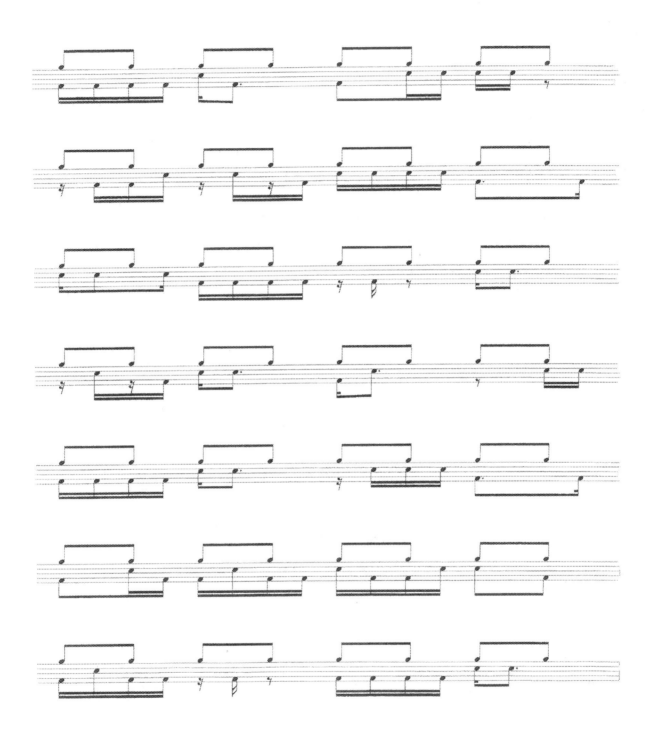

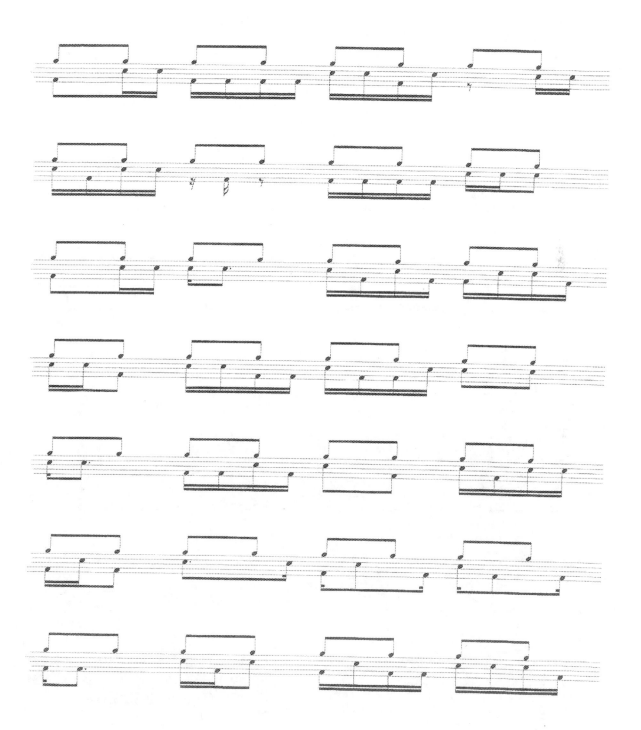

41

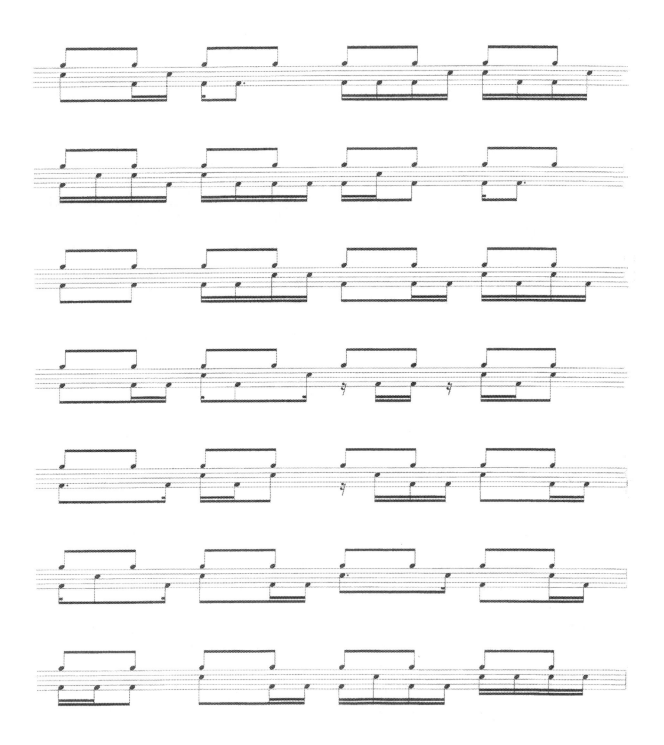

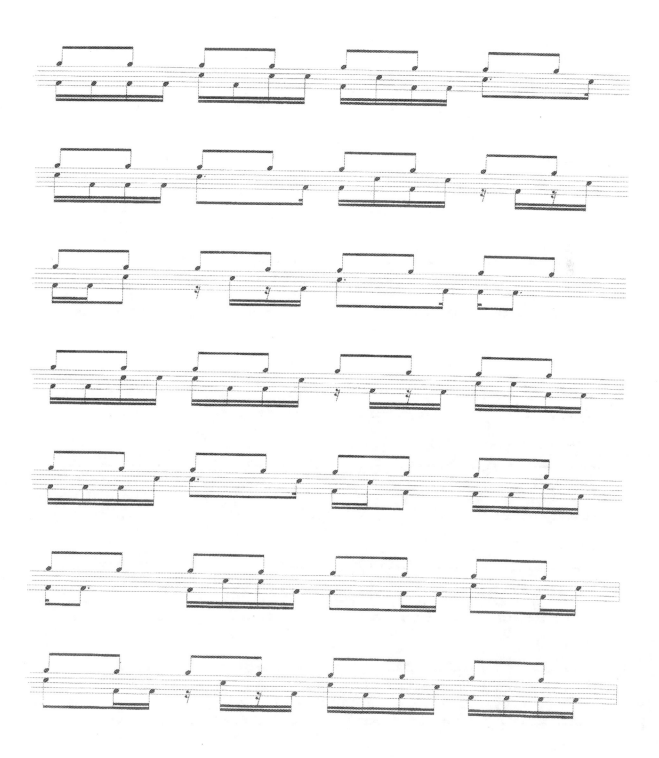

43

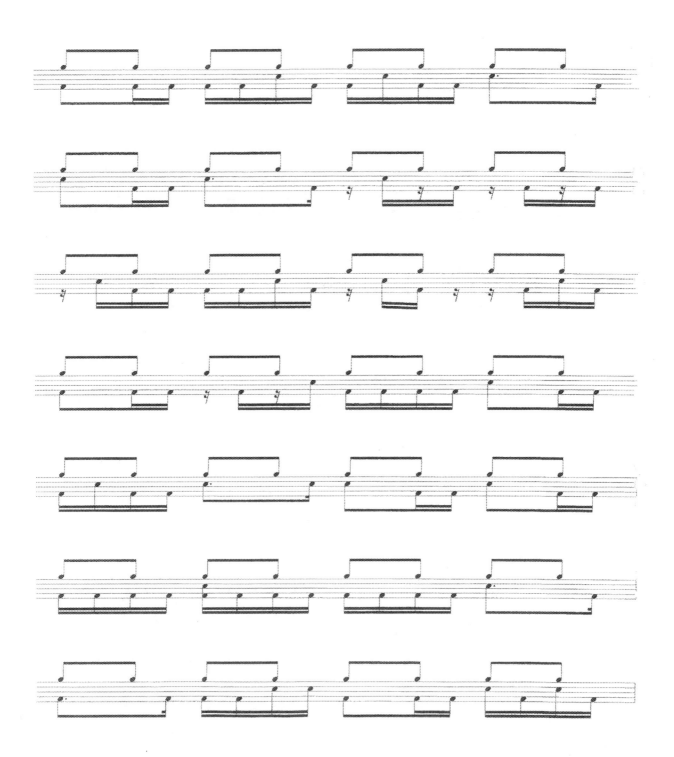

44

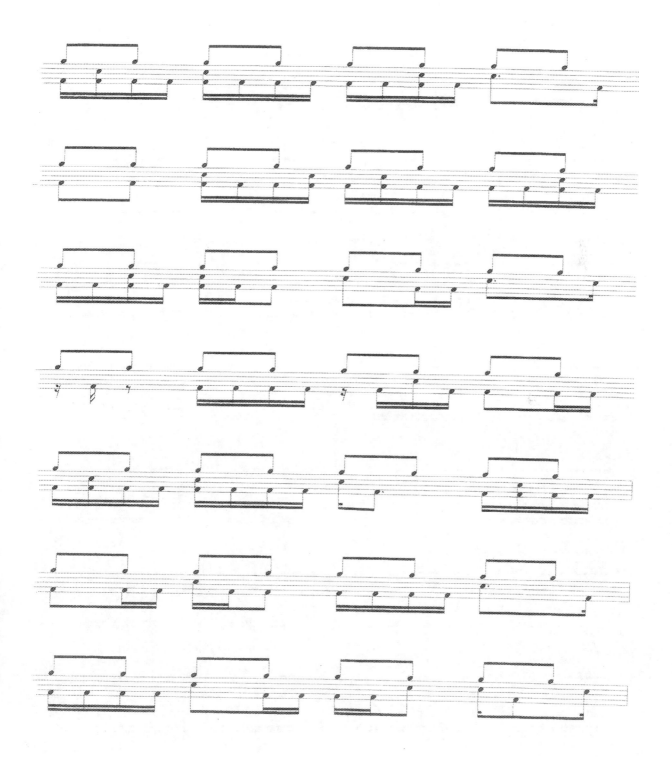

45

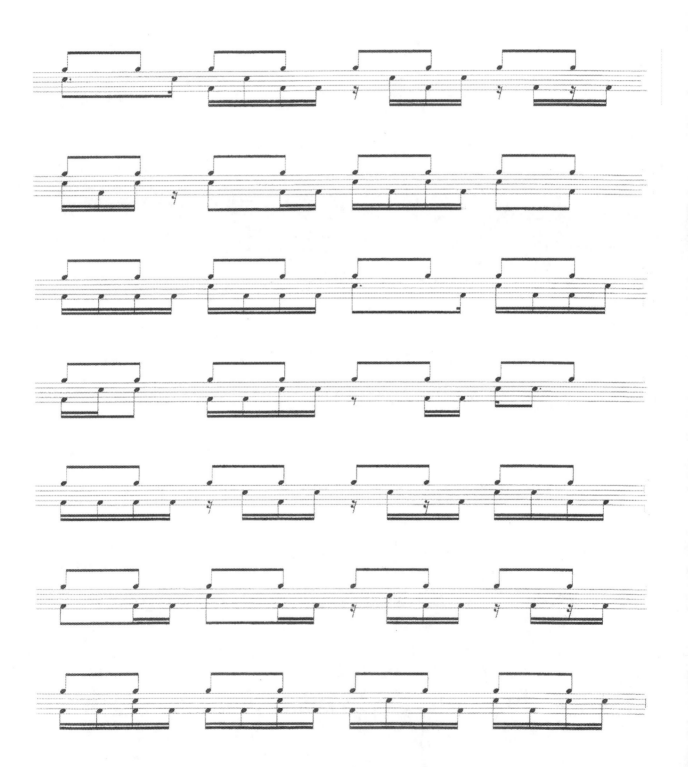

46

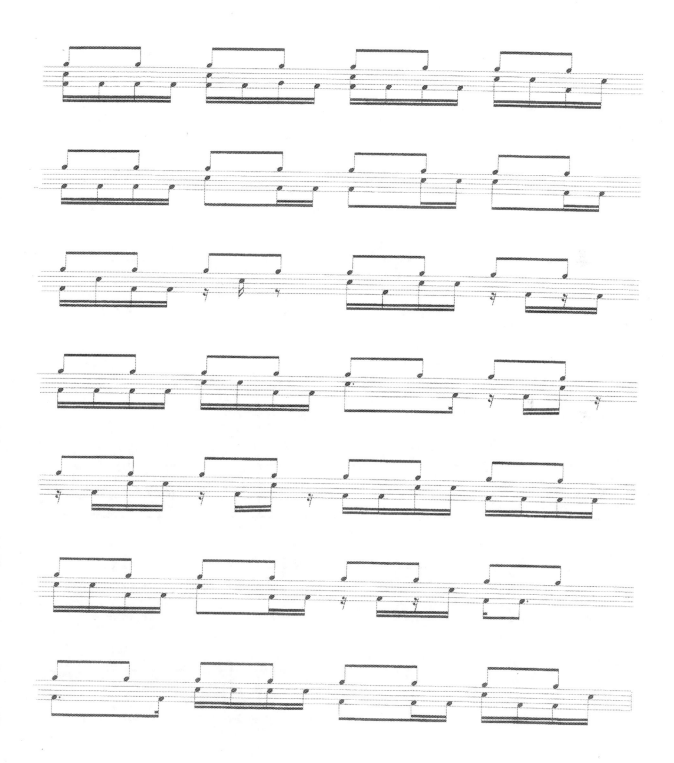

47

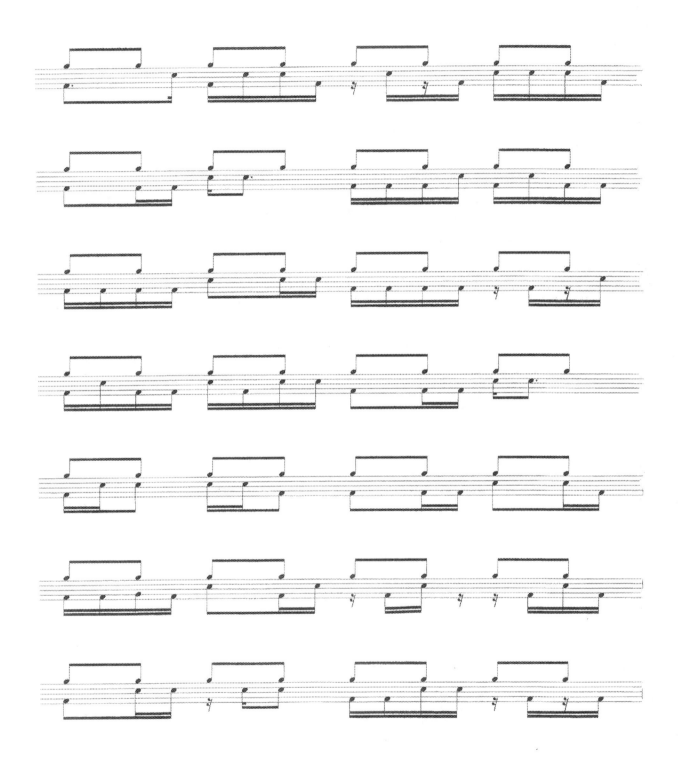

48

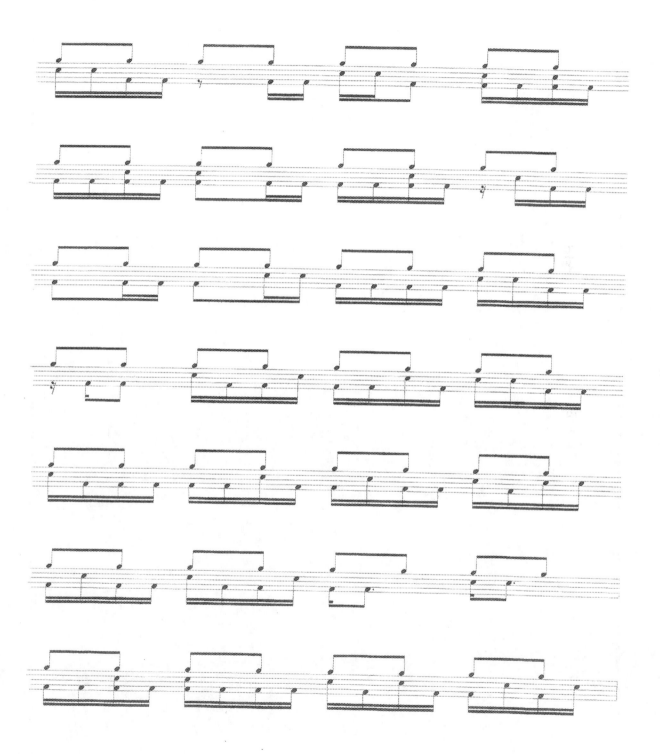

A drummer is only as good as his or her last performance!

1/16 Disco Rock Beats

1/16 NOTE DISCO ROCK BEATS

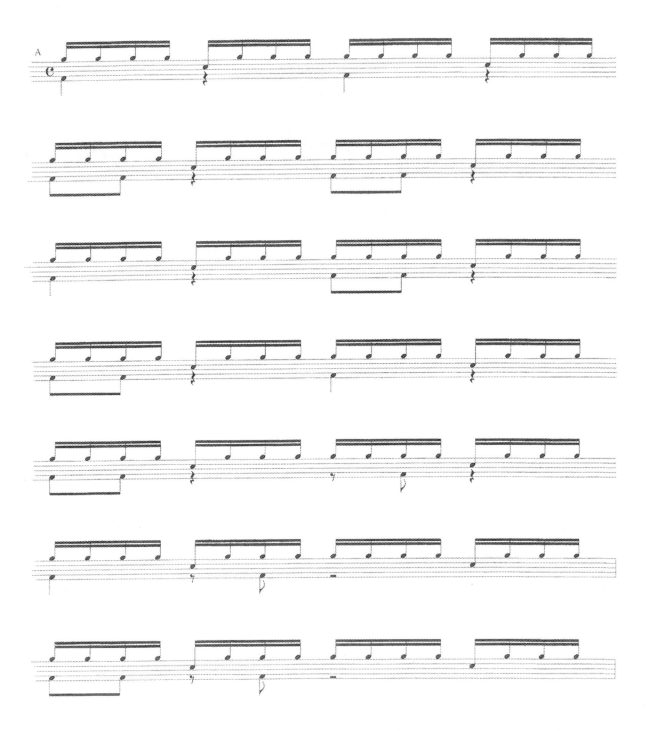

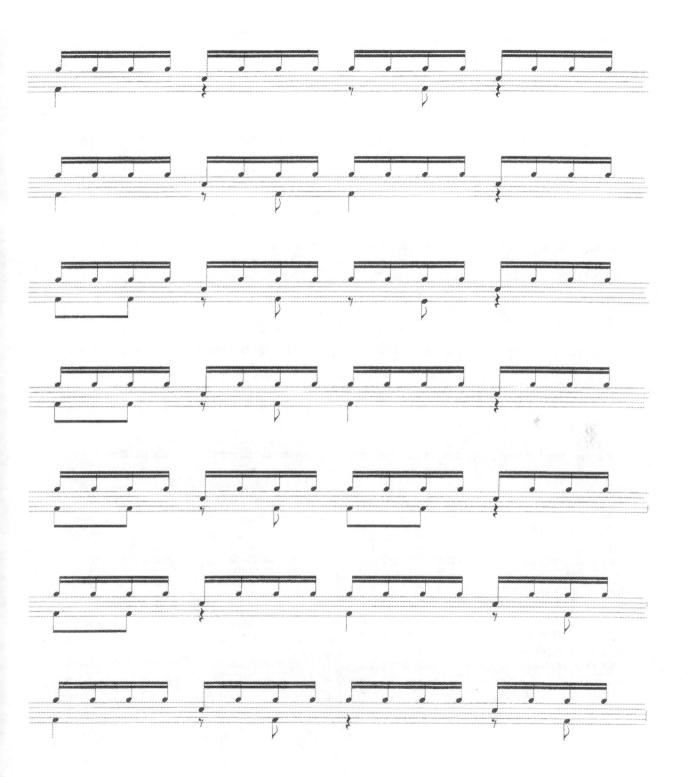

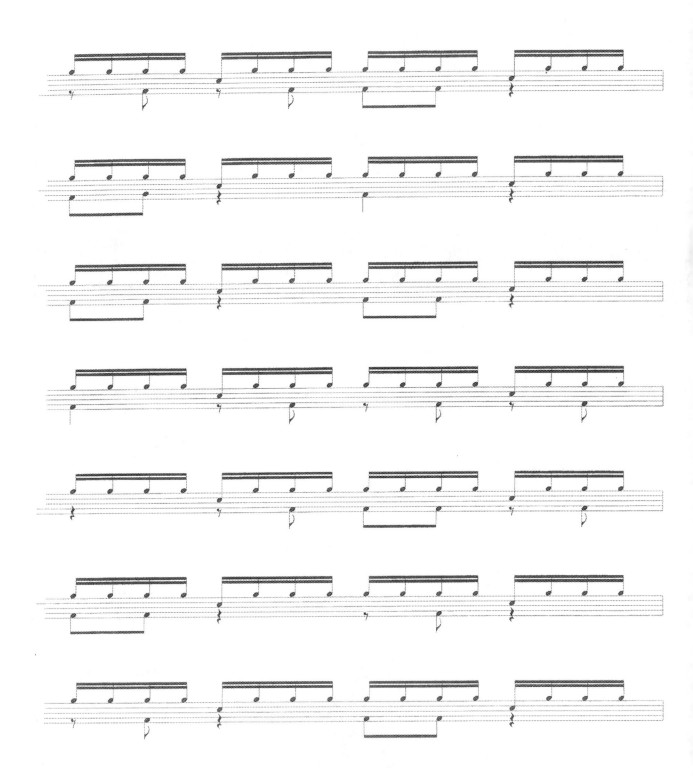

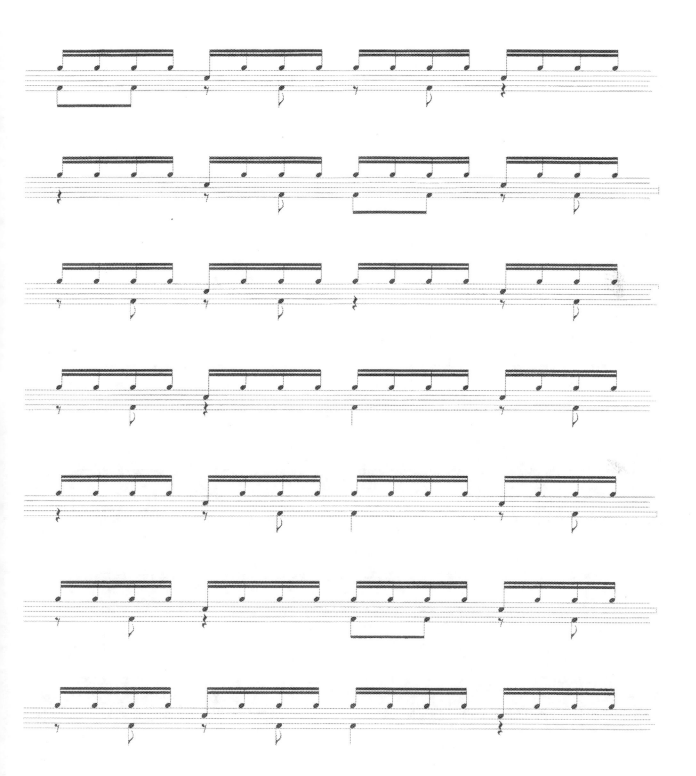

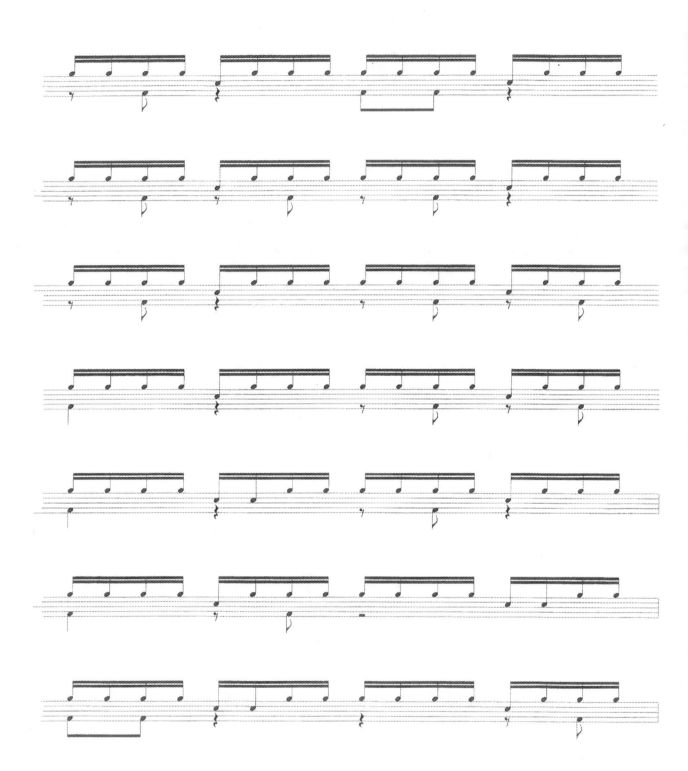

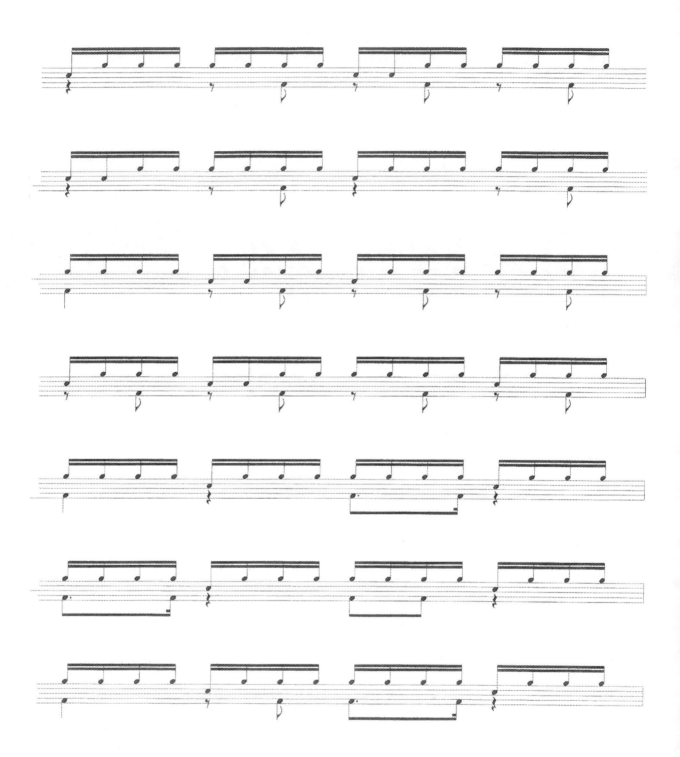

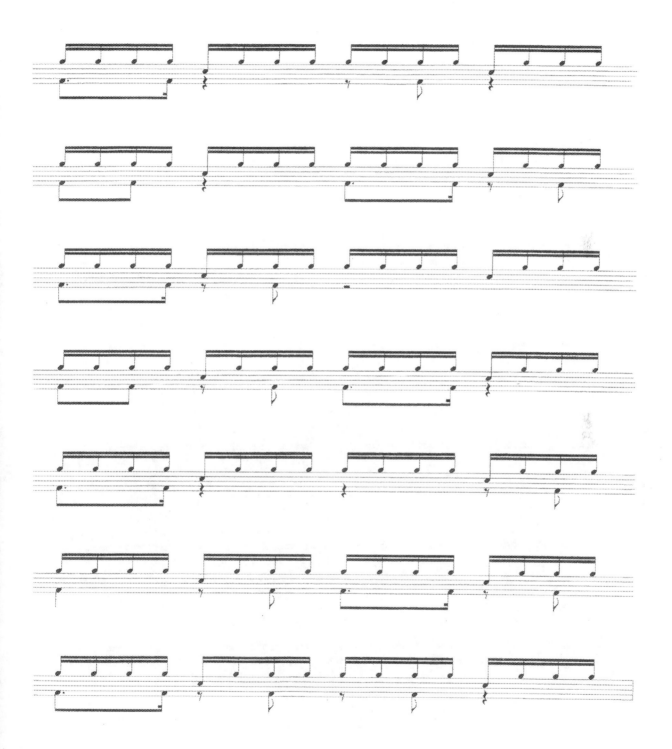

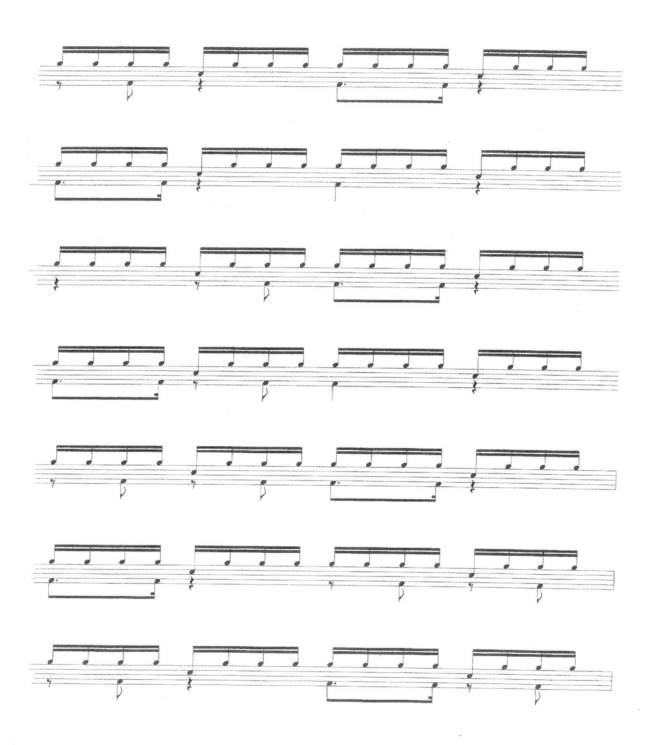

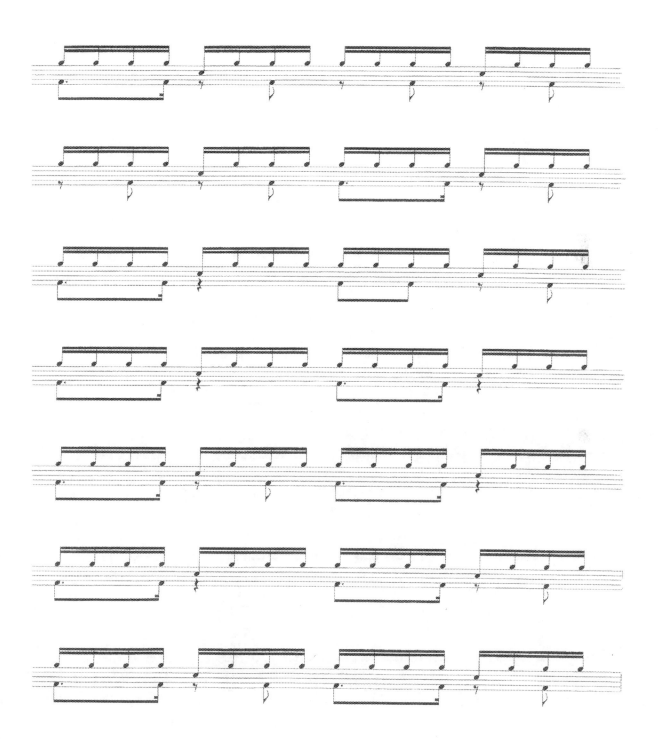

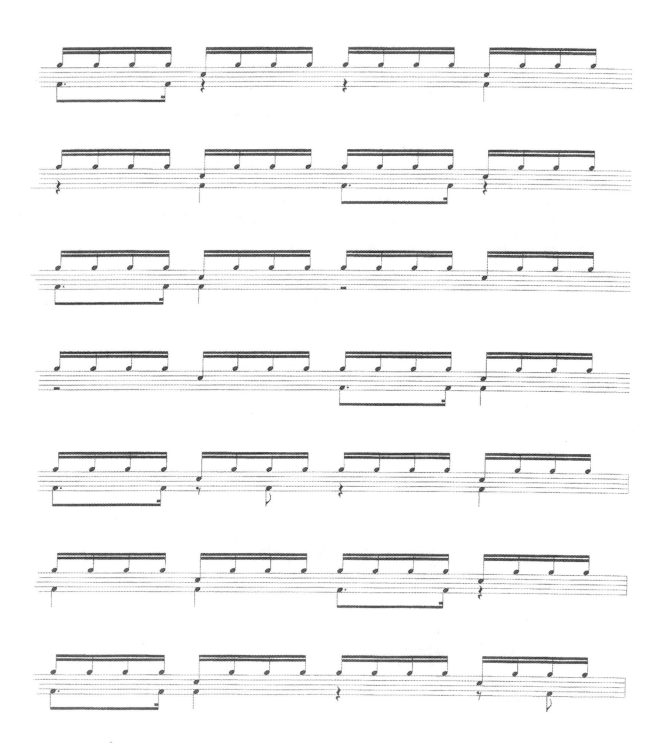

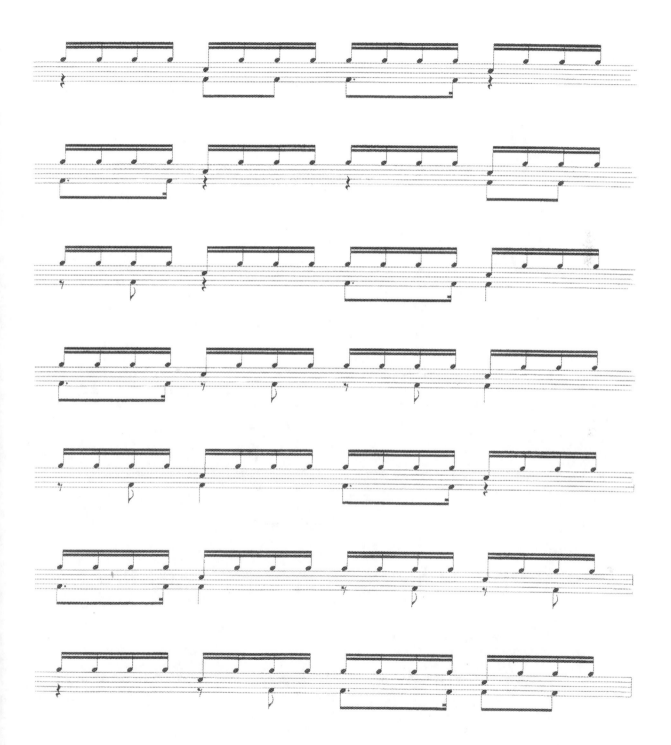

1/16 NOTE DISCO ROCK BEATS
PART 2

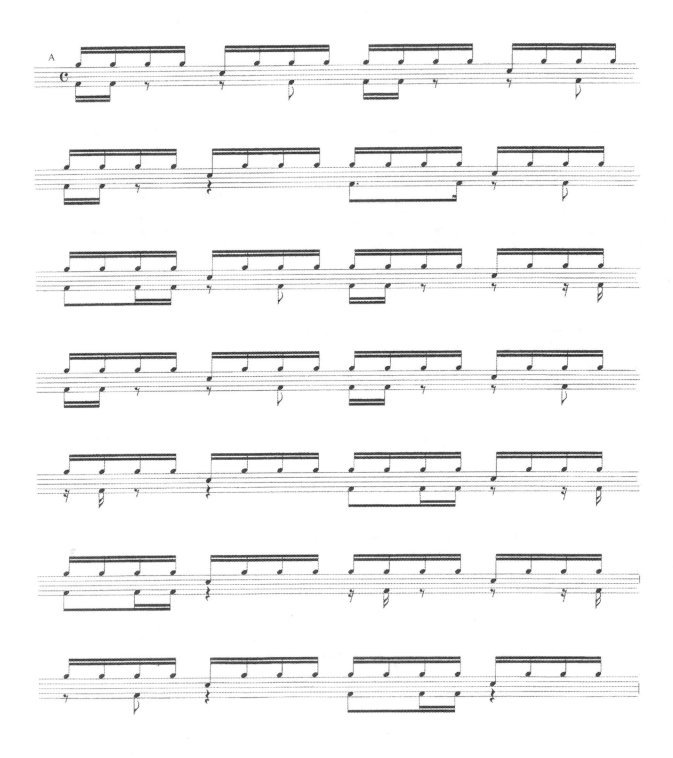

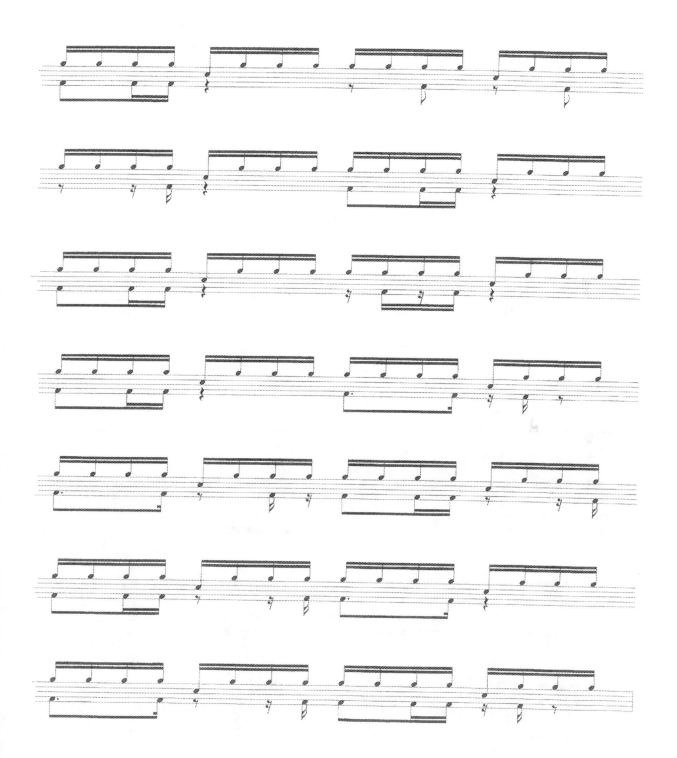

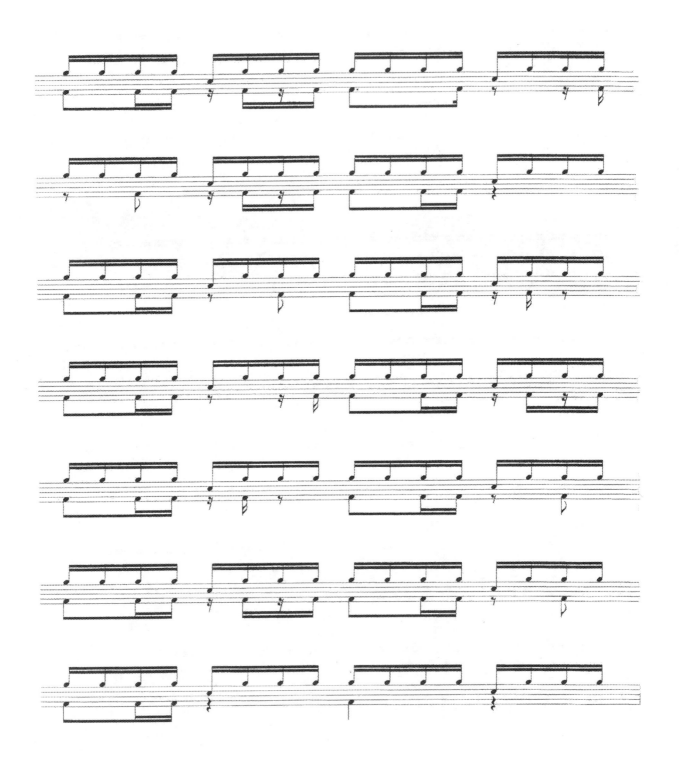

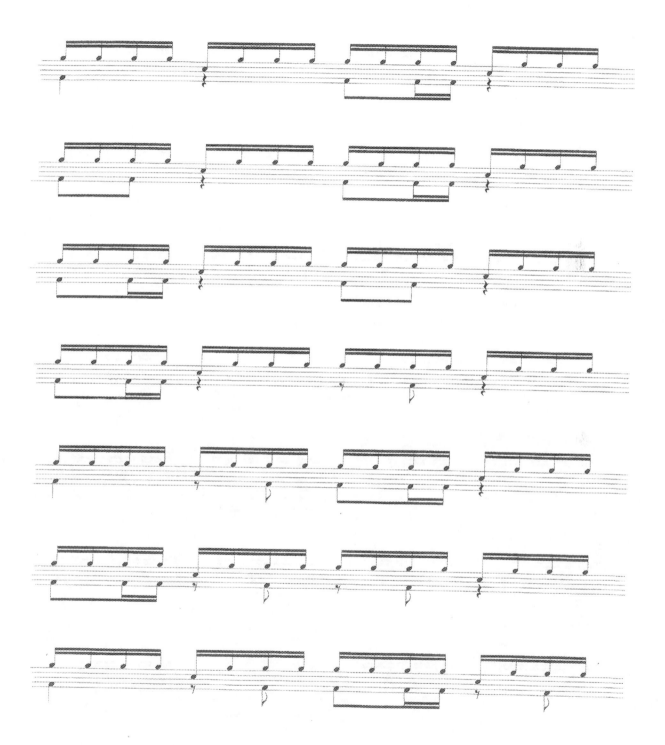

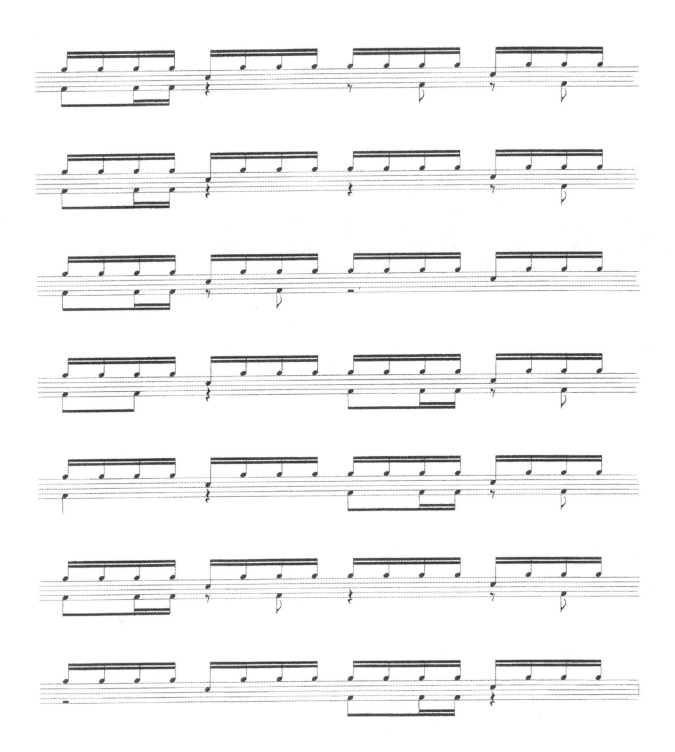

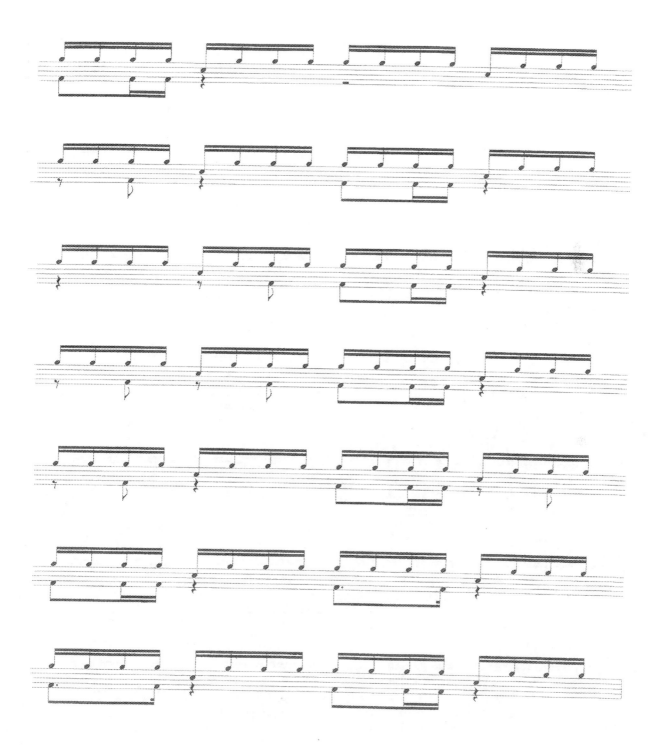

69

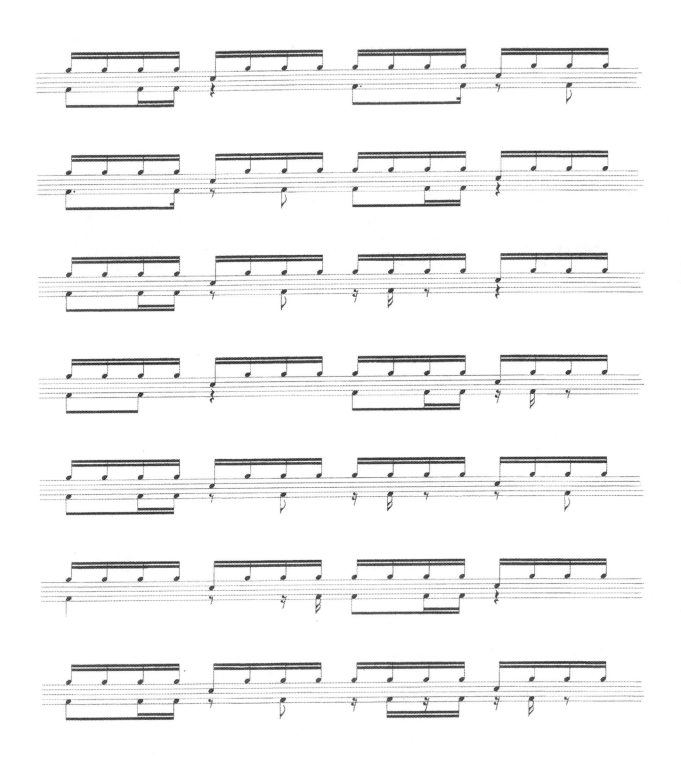

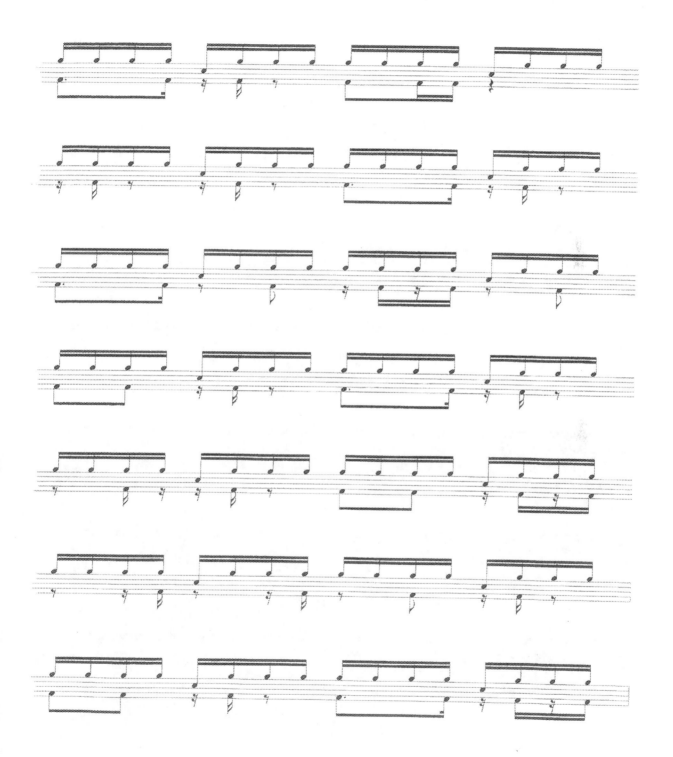

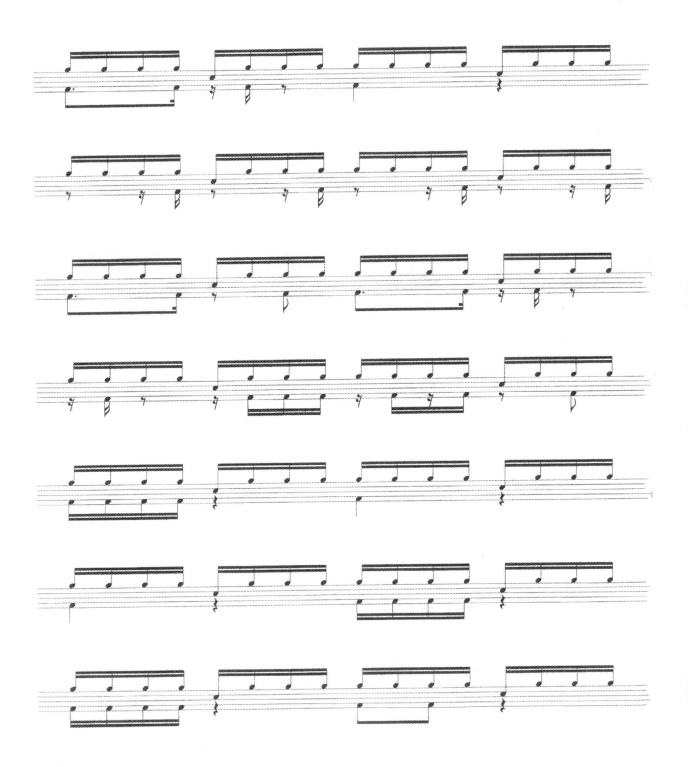

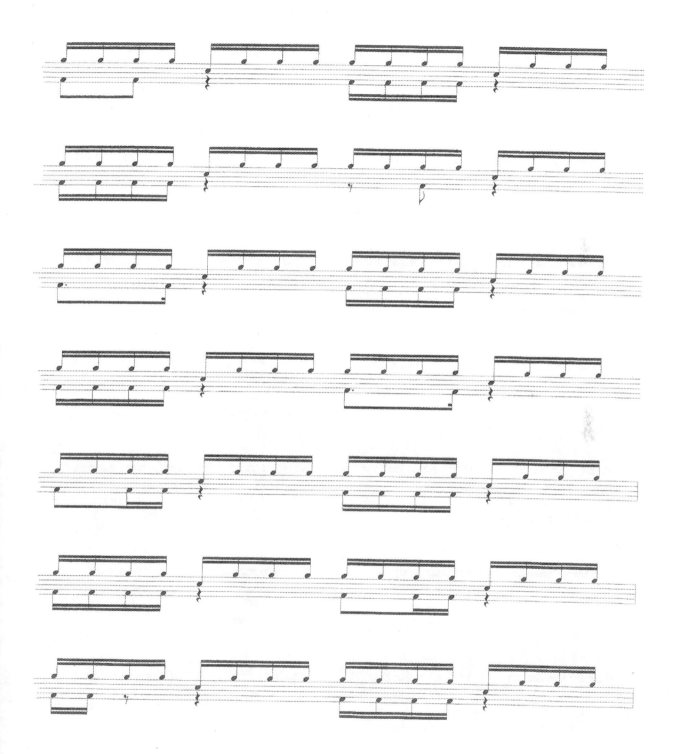

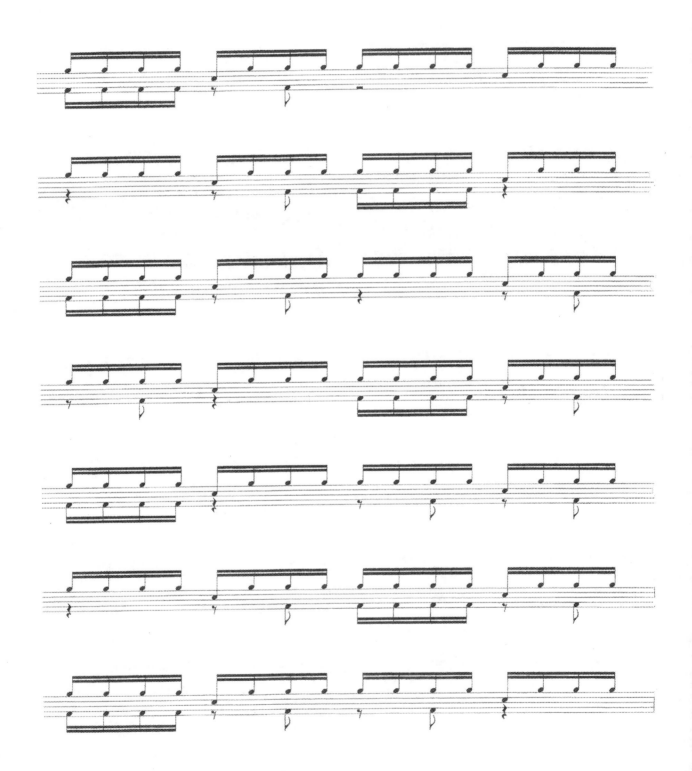

74

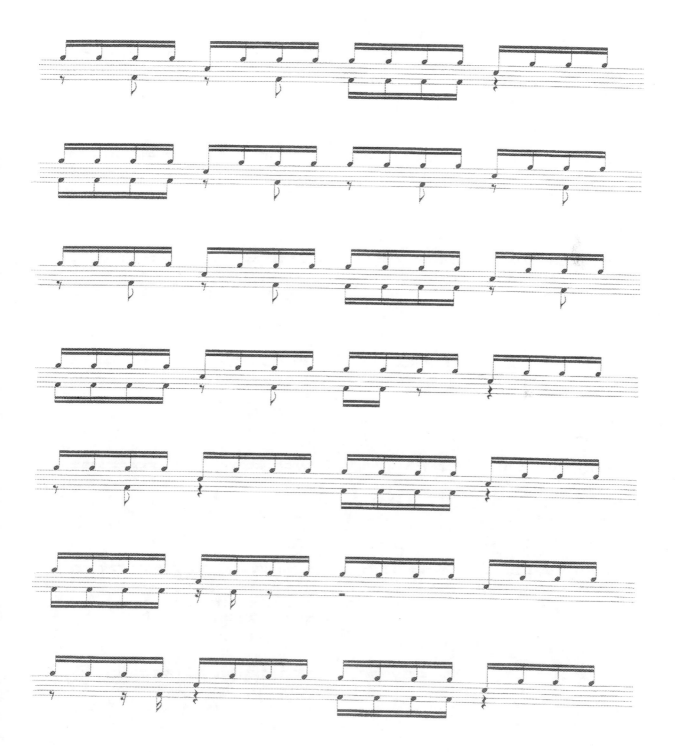

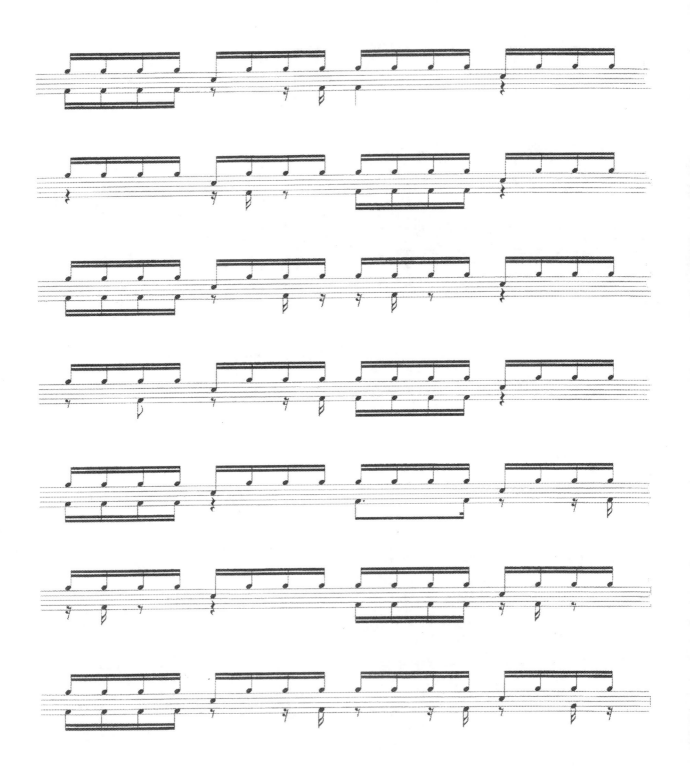

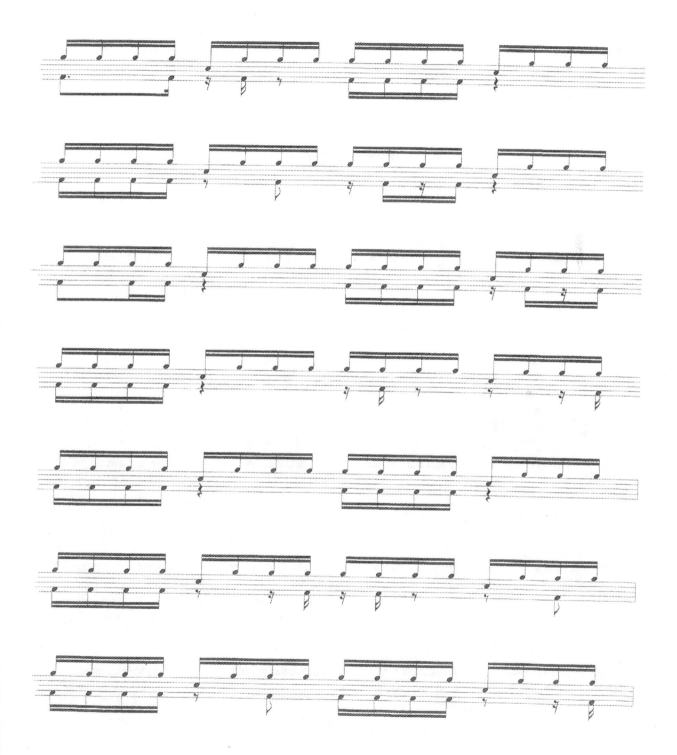

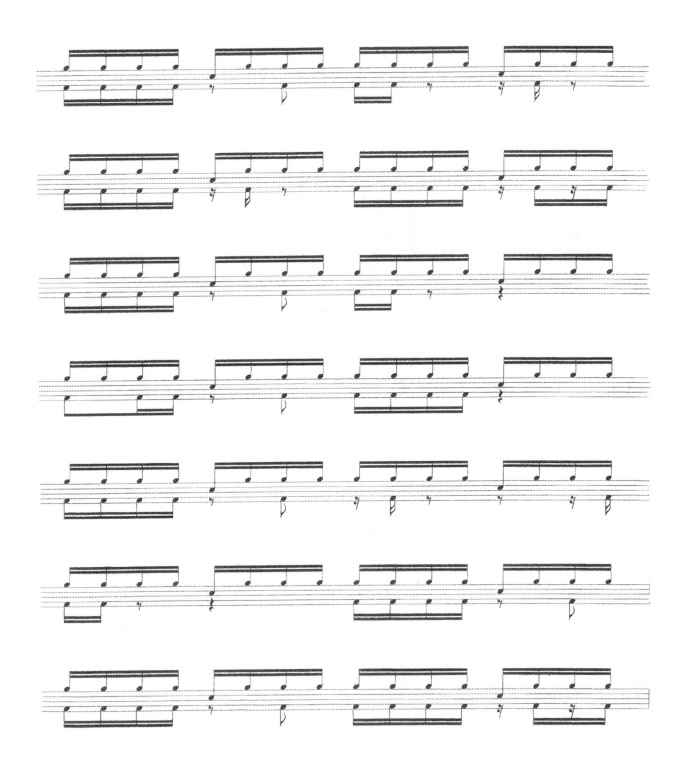

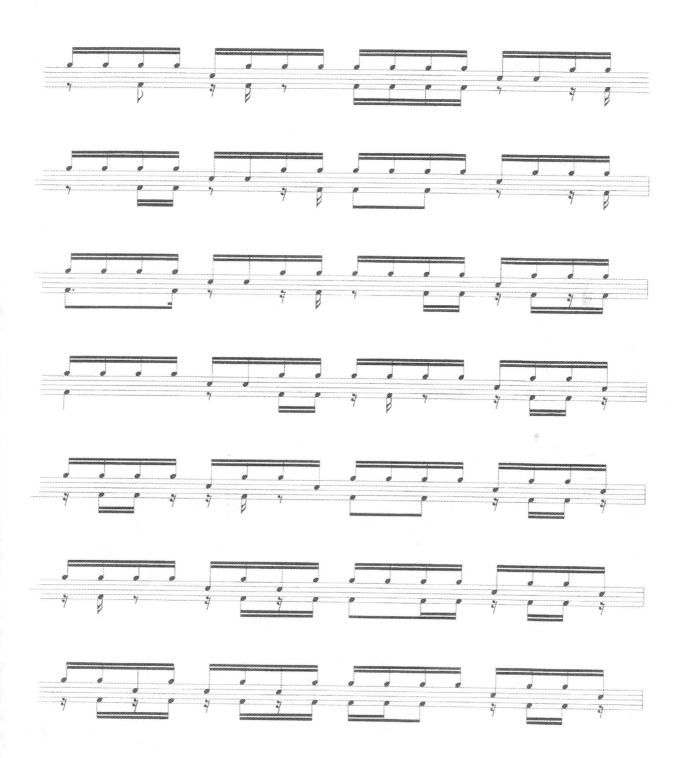

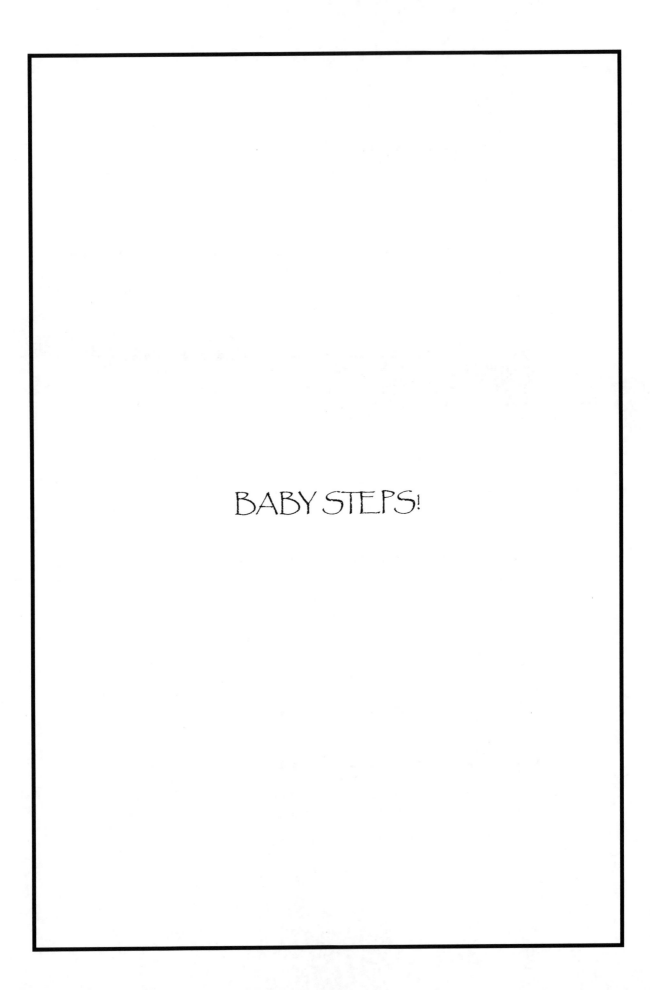

BABY STEPS!

1/16 One Handed Beats

1/16 NOTE ONE HANDED BEATS

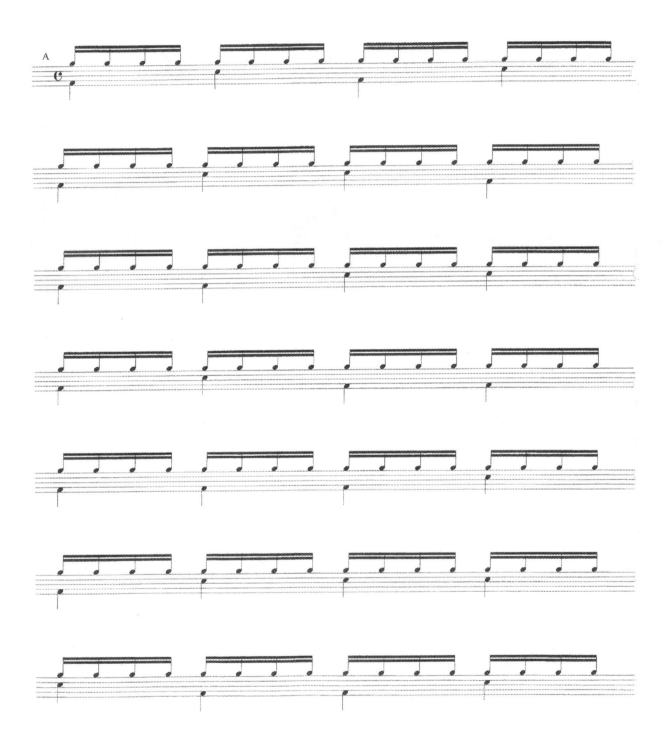

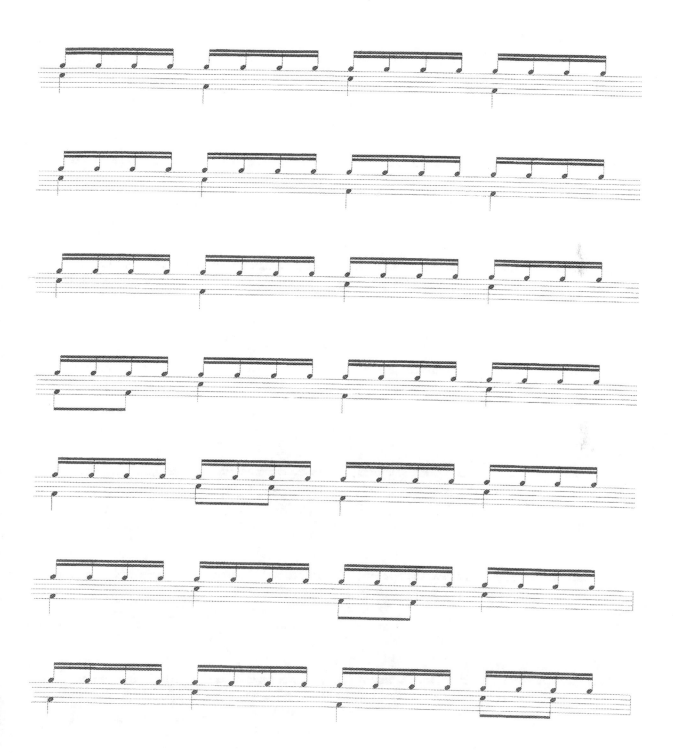

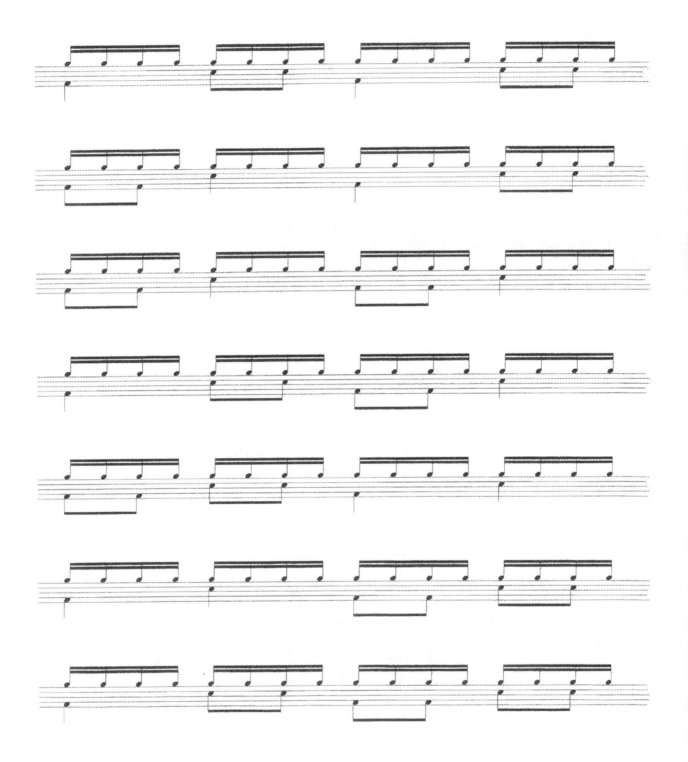

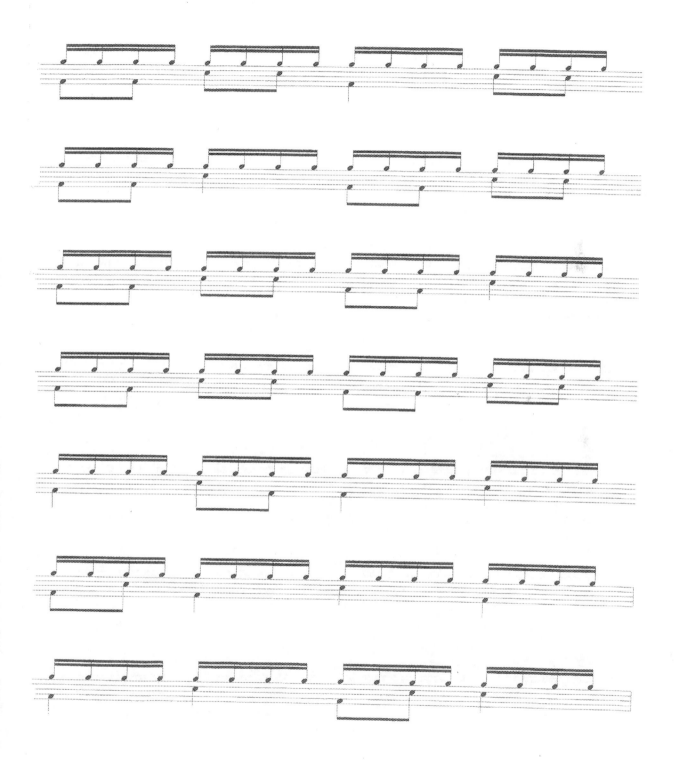

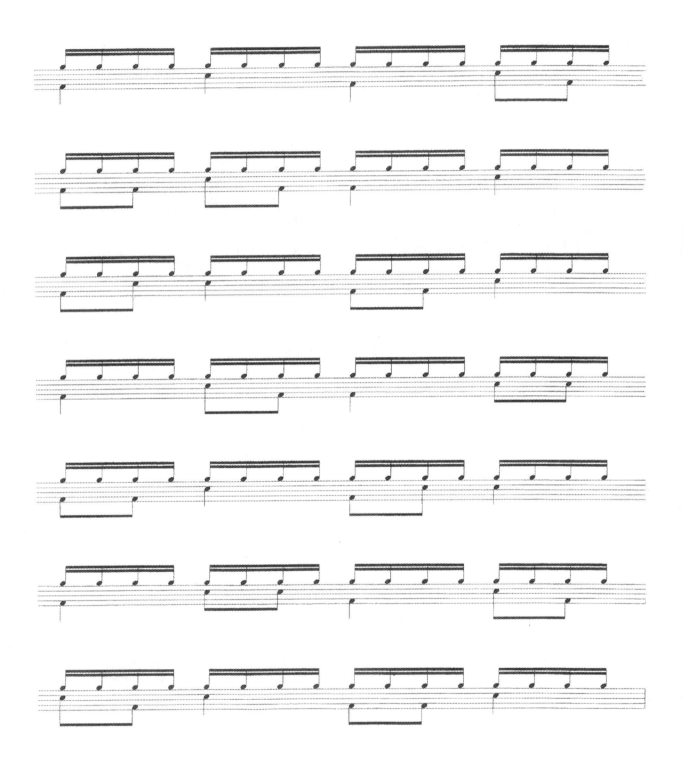

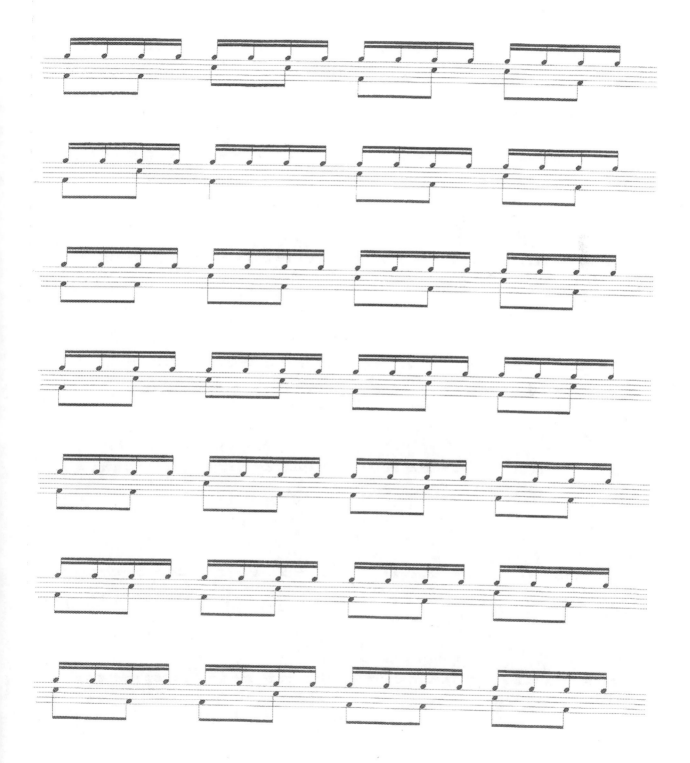

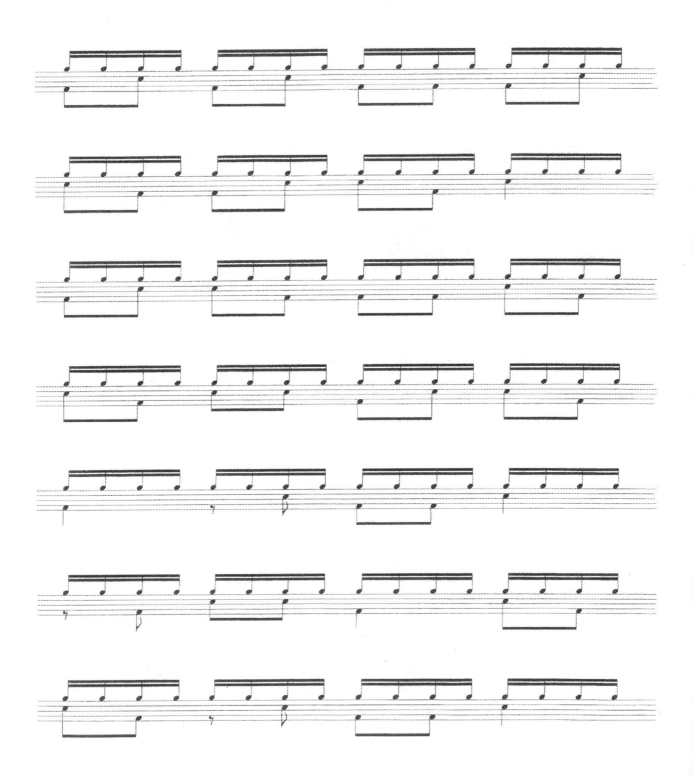

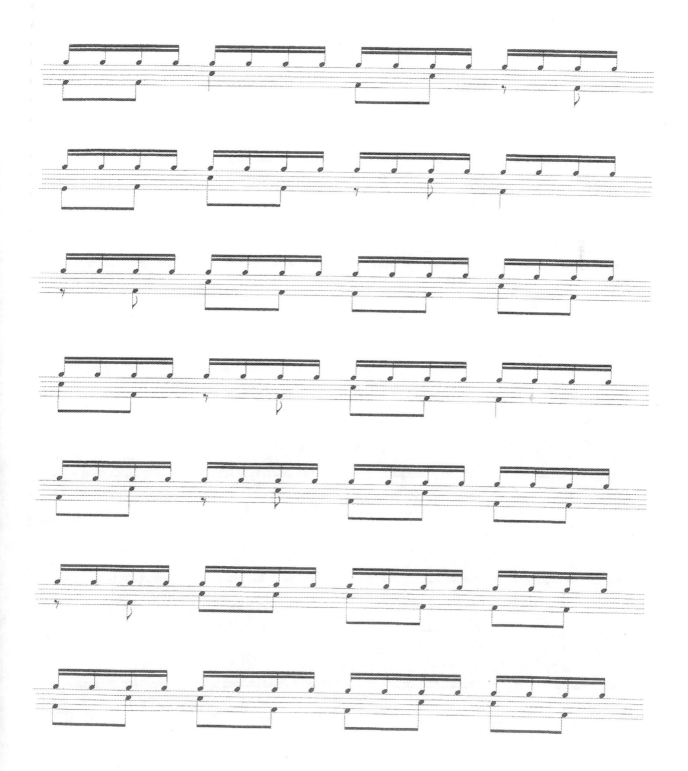

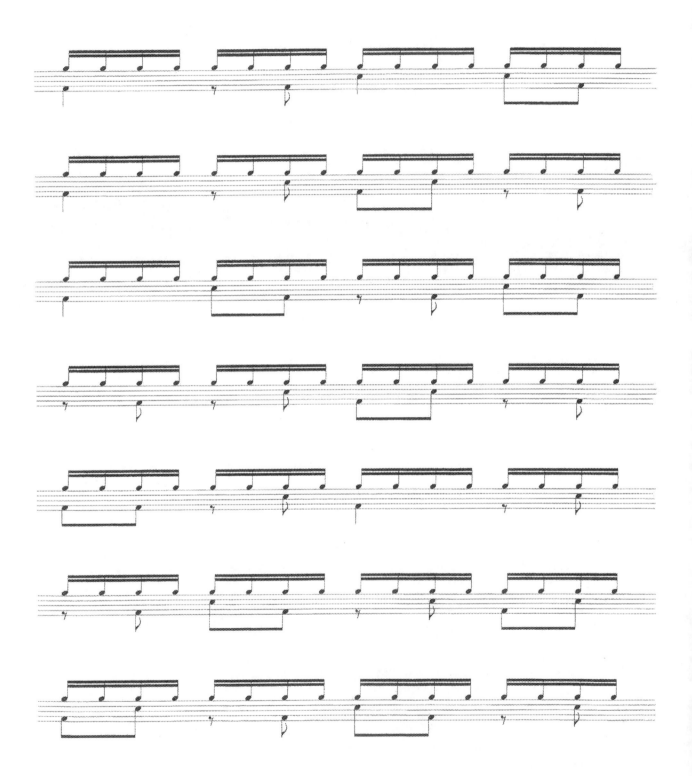

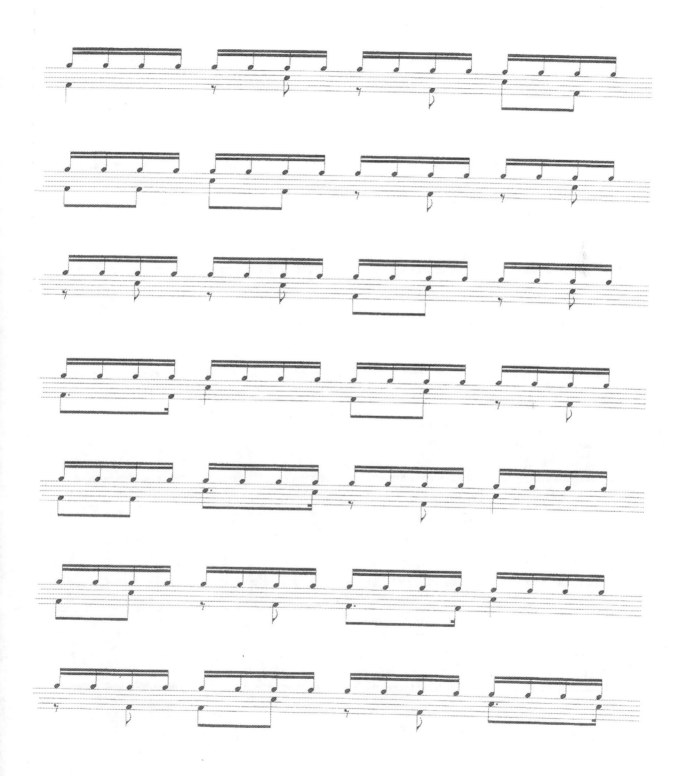

91

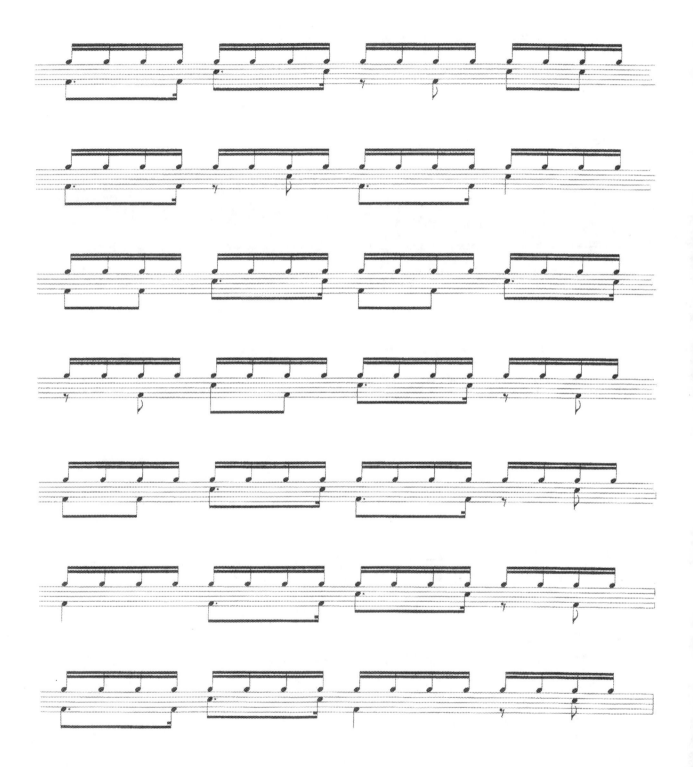

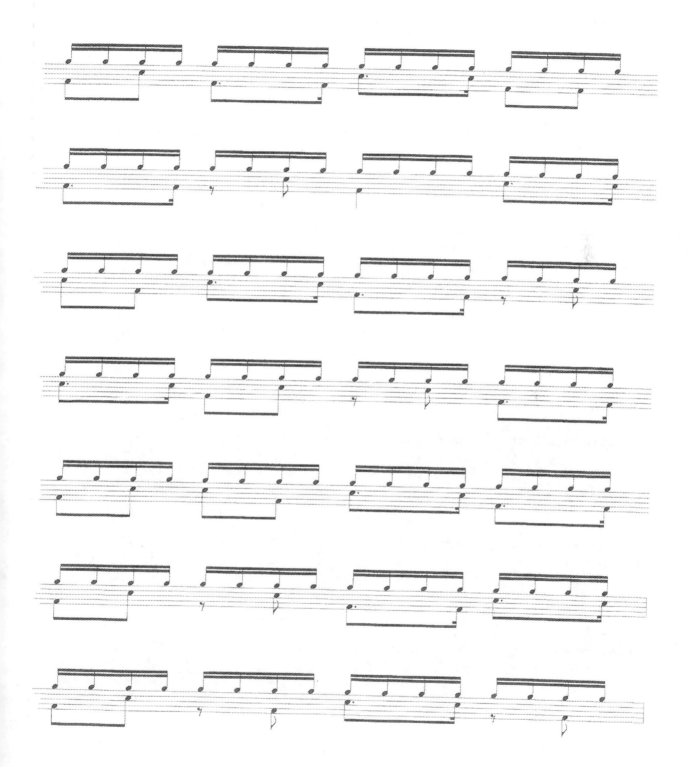

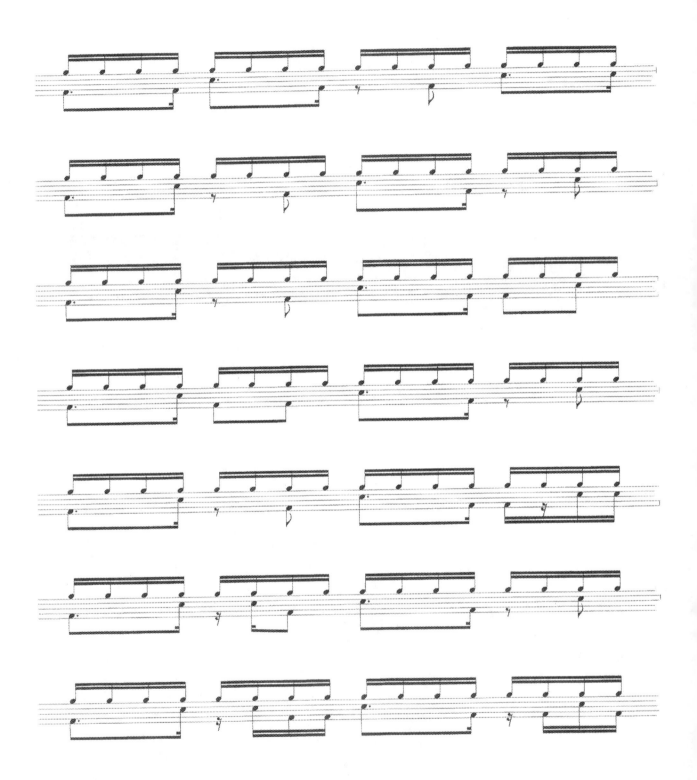

94

1/16 NOTE ONE HANDED BEATS
PART 2

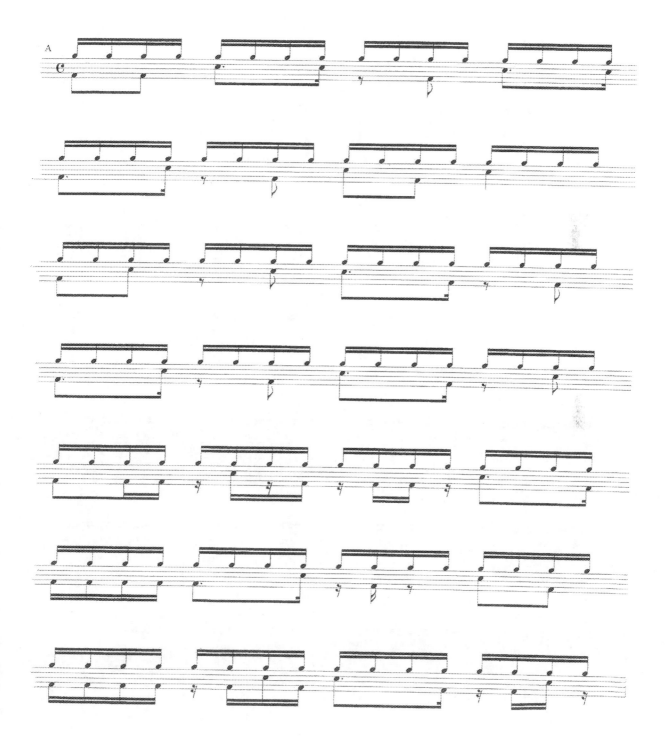

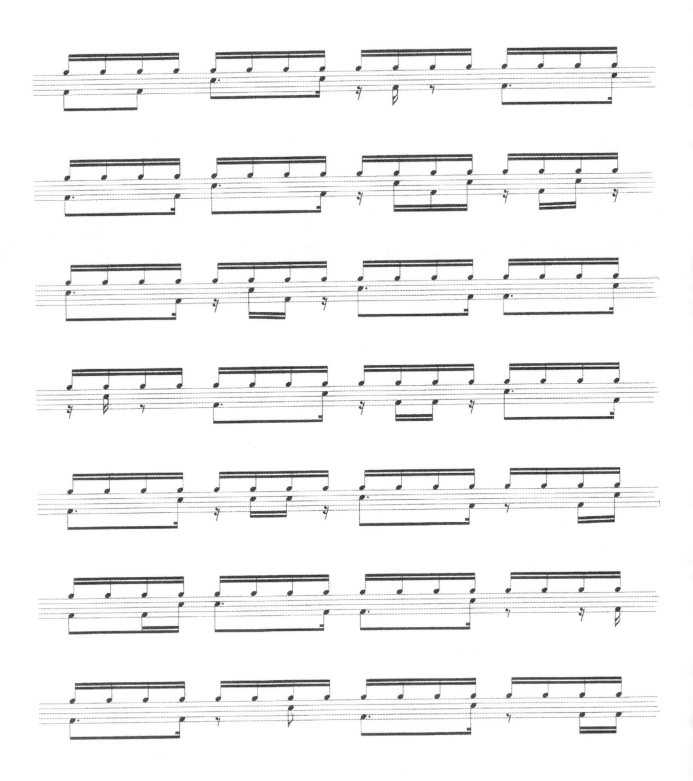

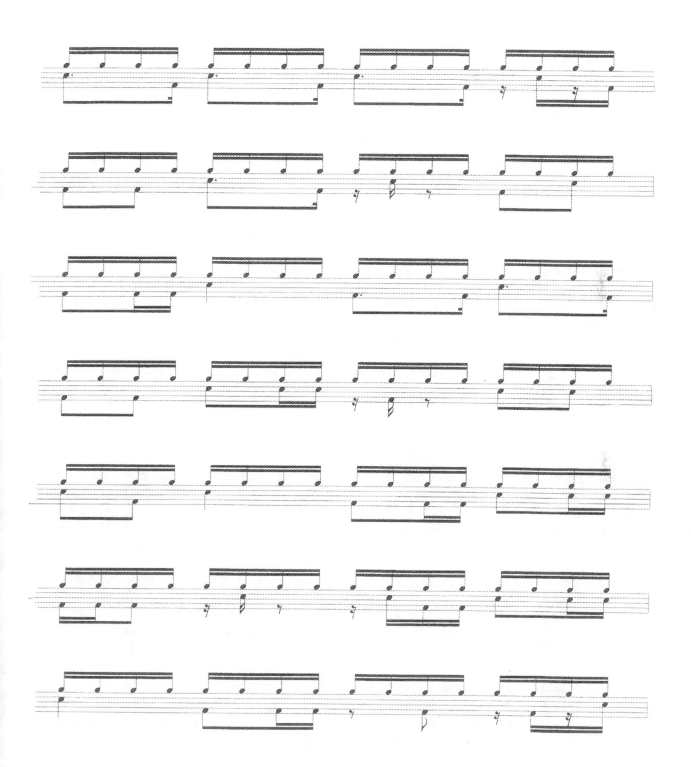

97

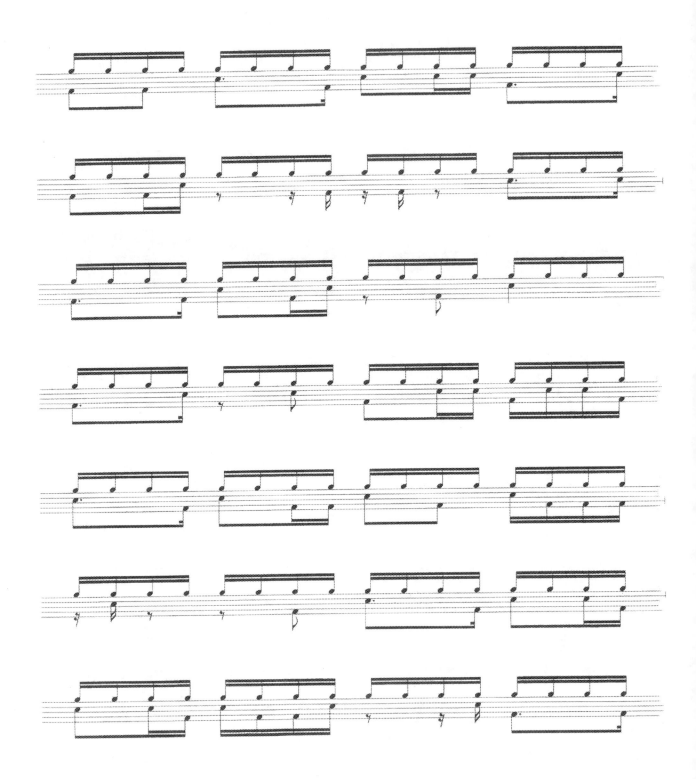

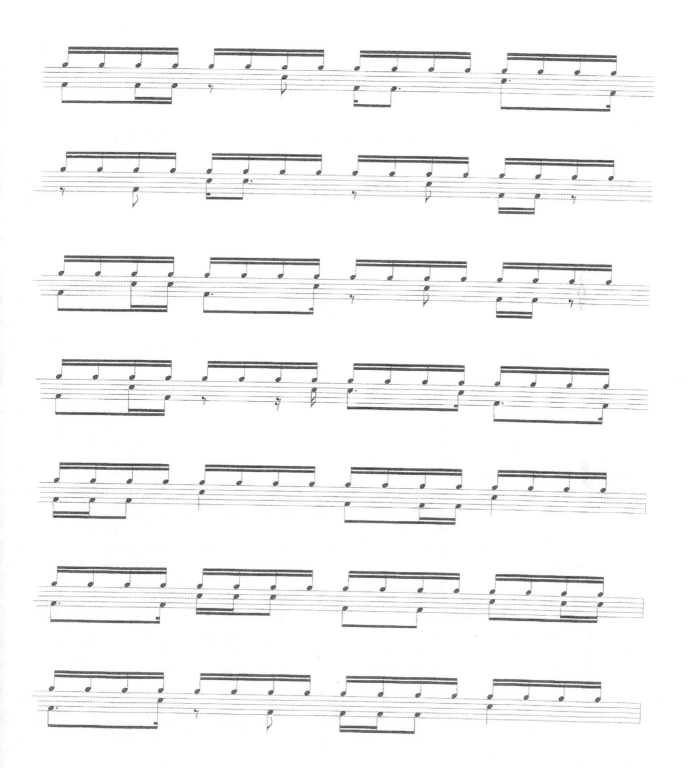

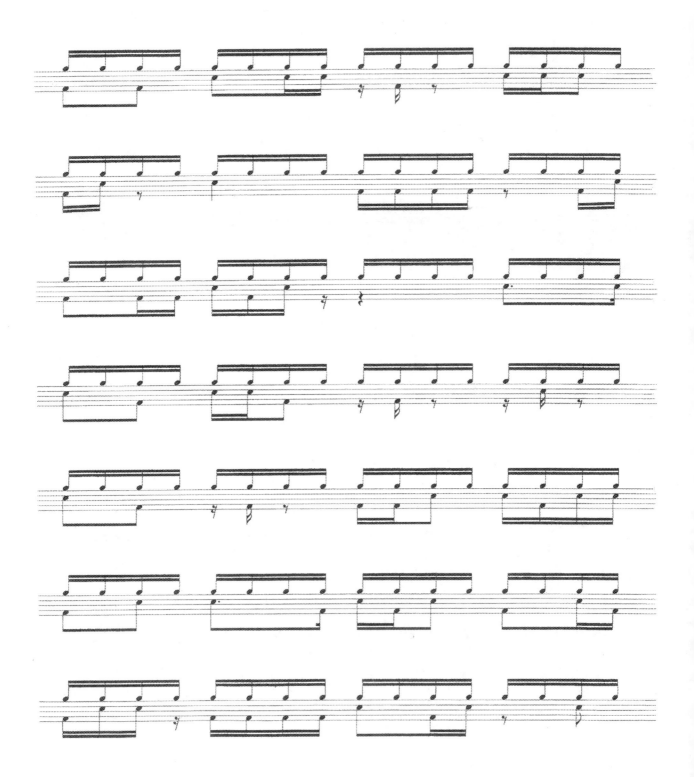

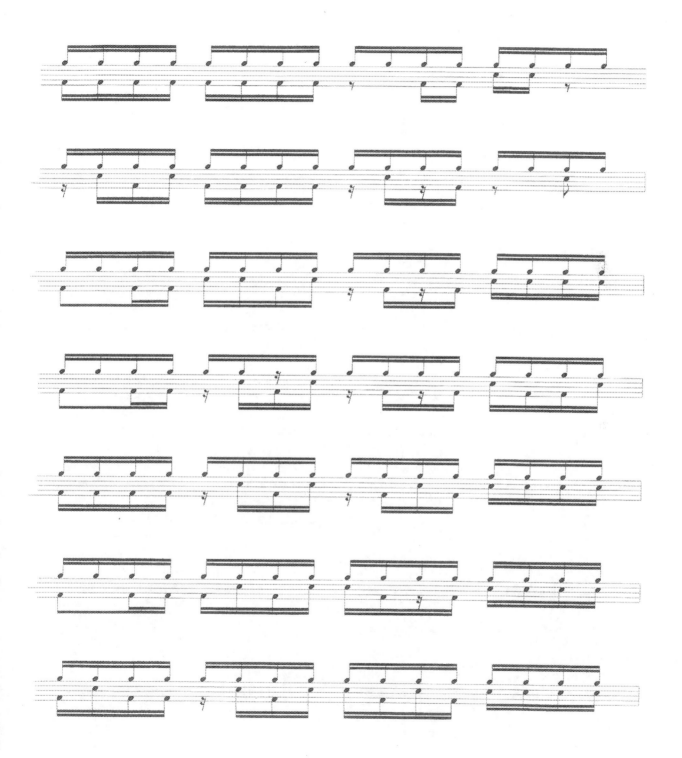

1/16 NOTE ONE HANDED BEATS
PART 3

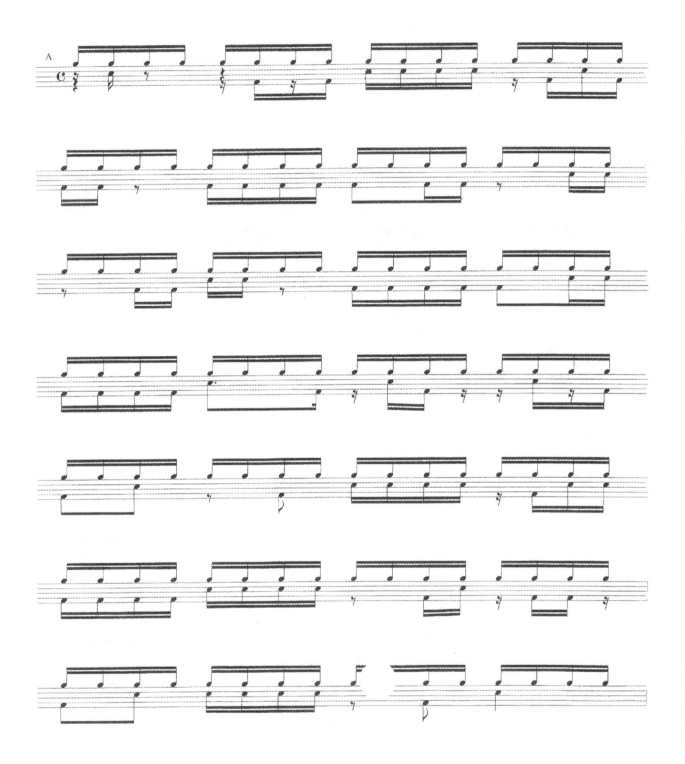

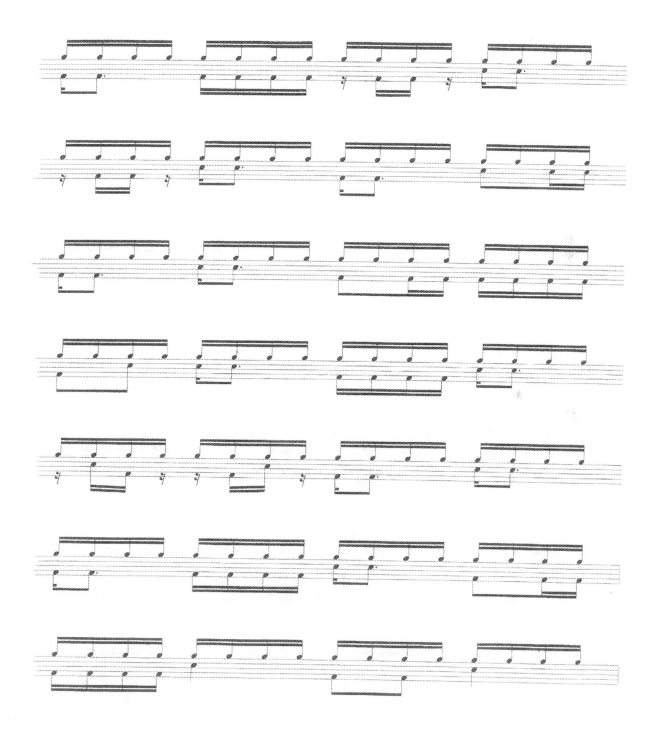

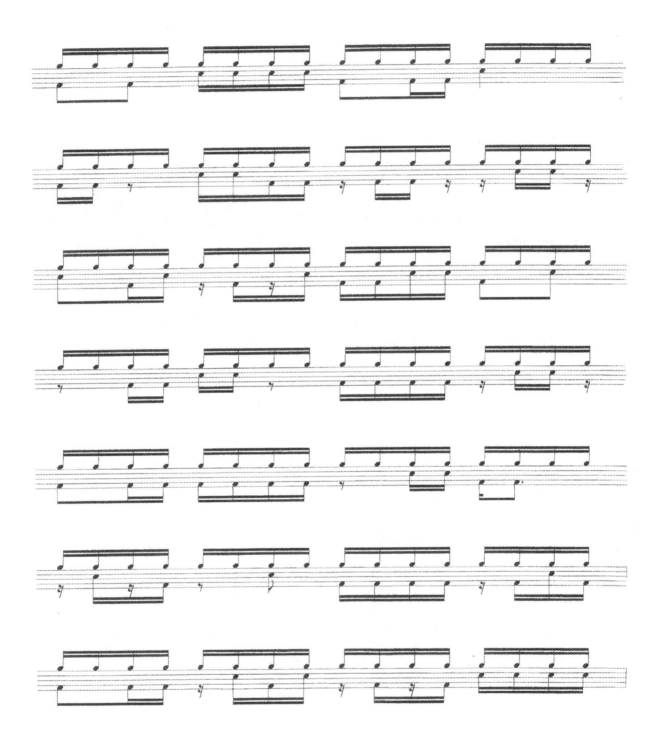

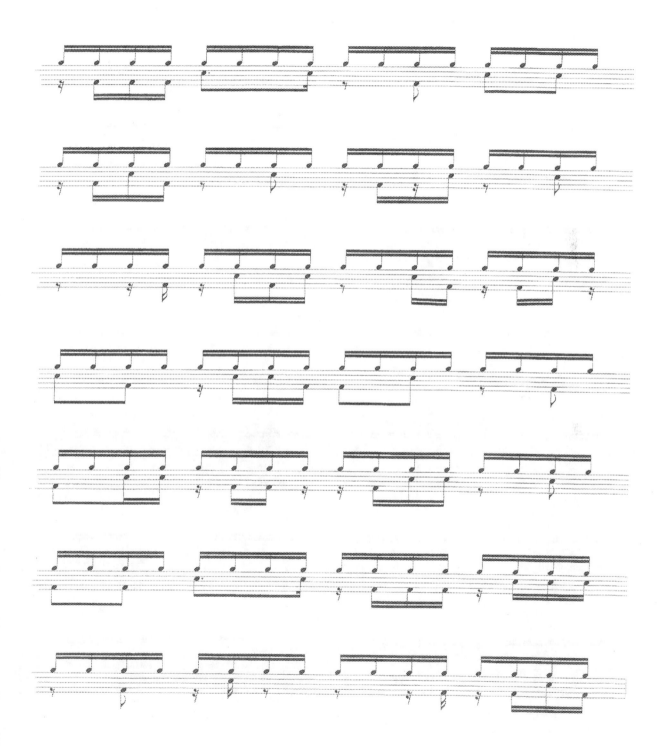

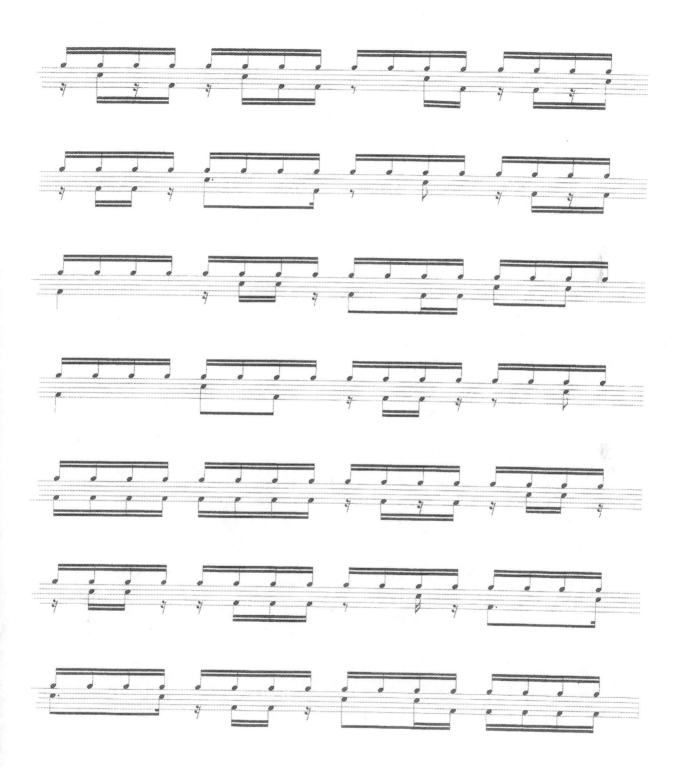

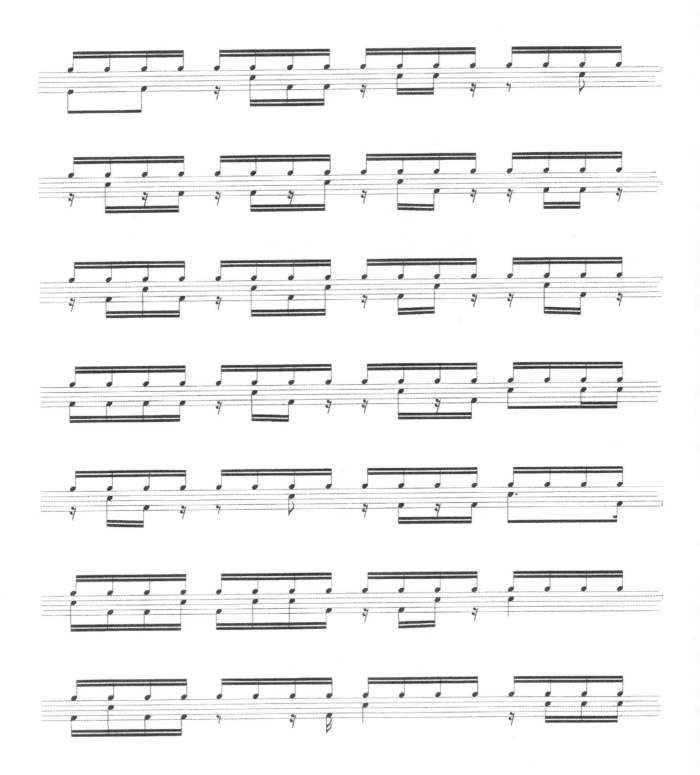

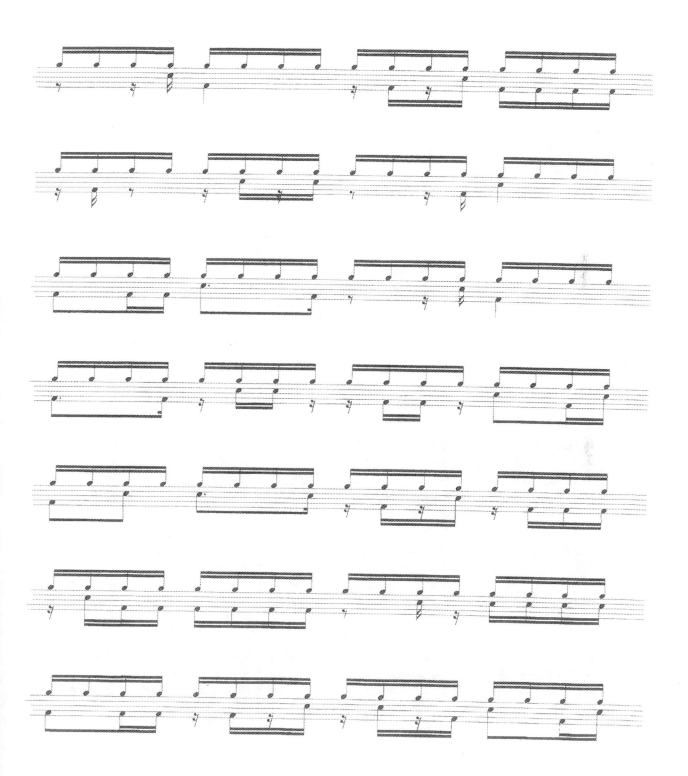

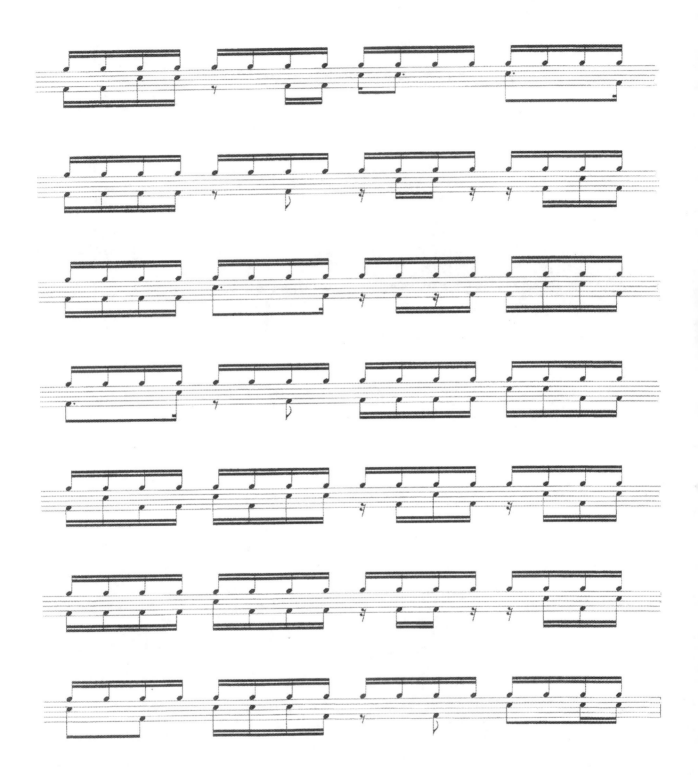

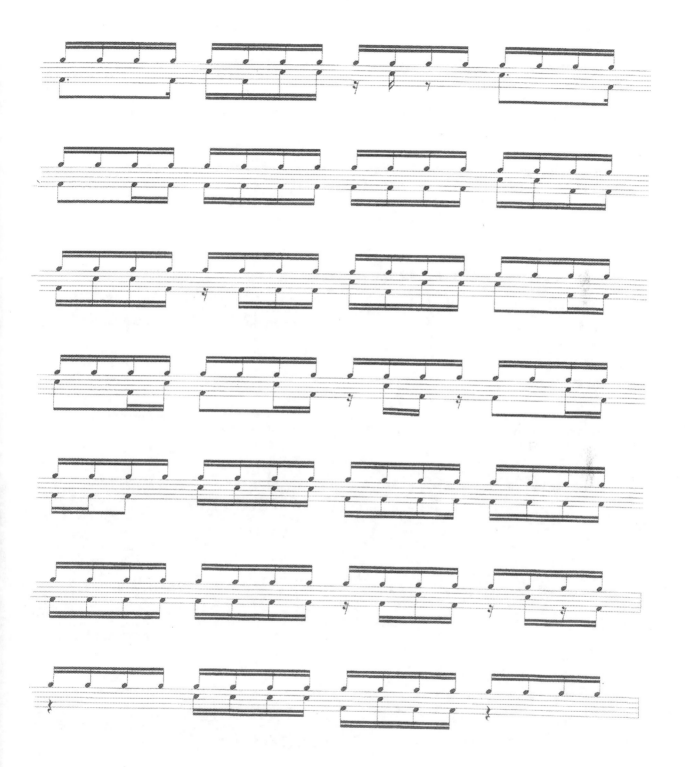

112

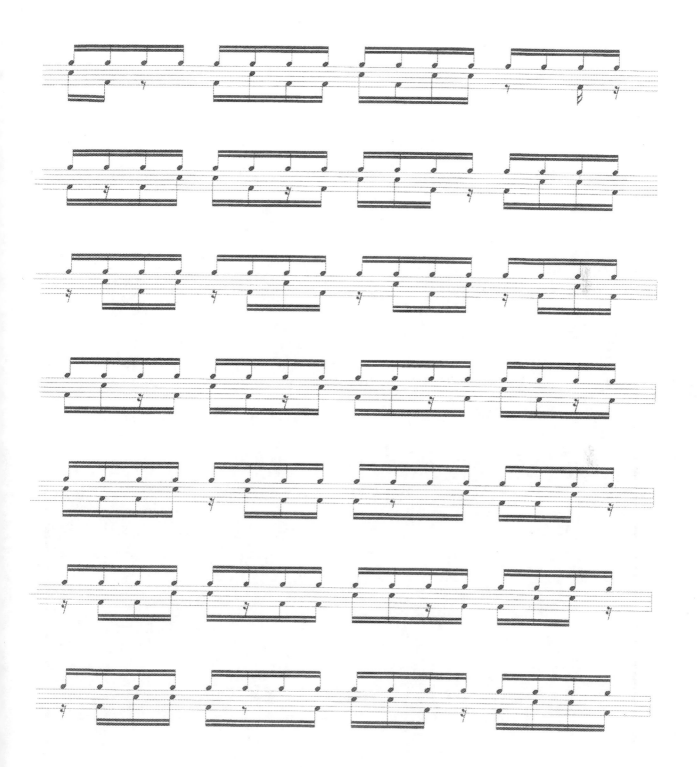

113

The great things in life are difficult because if they weren't, they wouldn't be so great!

Crash Book

CRASHBOOK

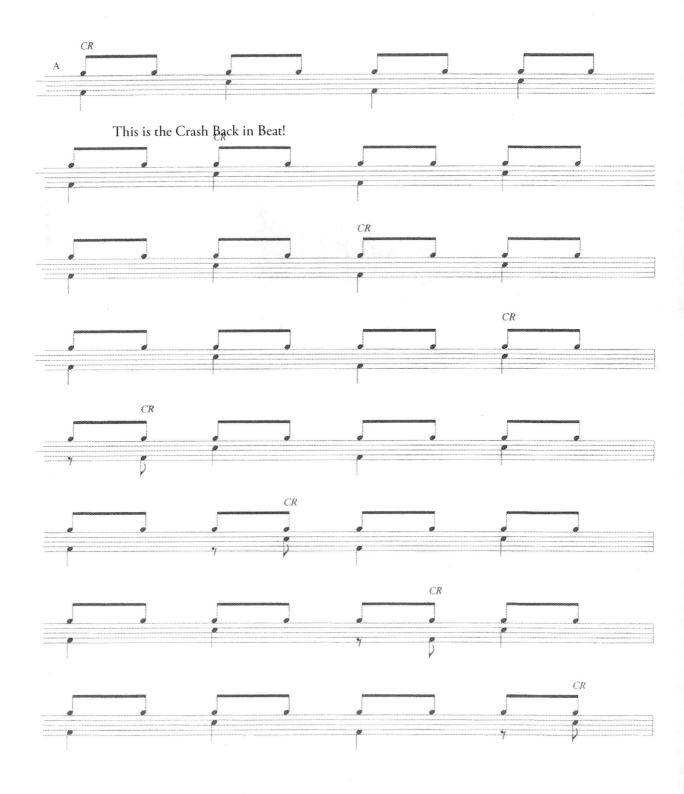

This is the Crash Back in Beat!

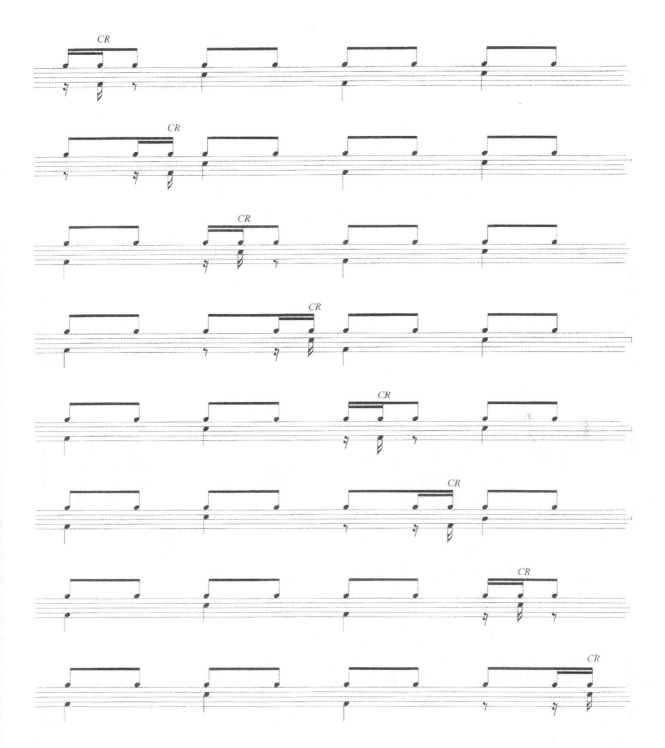

Three Types of Crashing

1. <u>Directional:</u> This is the most important type of crashing! We are transitioning the band from one part of the song to another!
2. <u>Accental:</u> Crashing on accents with other members of the band!
3. Melodic: Crescendo symbols and any cymbal work playing along with the melody!

Playing fast doesn't make you a great
drummer, but playing efficiently will!

1 2 3 4 Fills

1/8 NOTE FILLS AND 1 2 3 4 FILLS

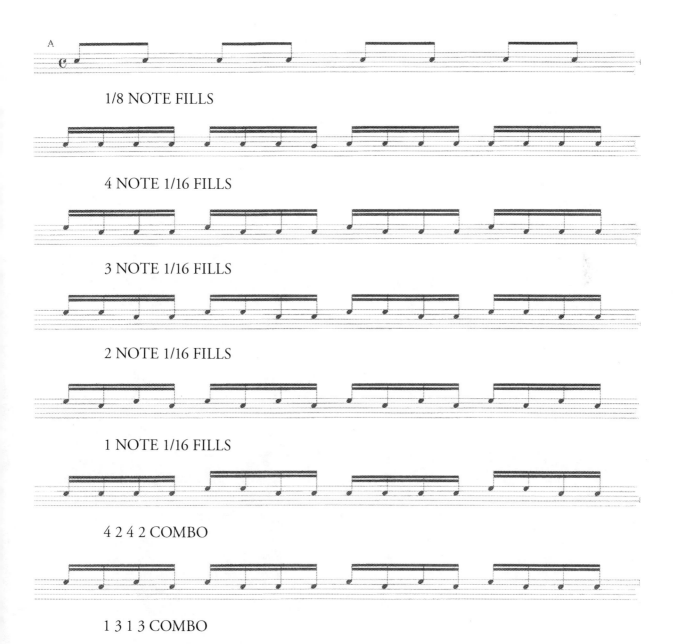

1/8 NOTE FILLS

4 NOTE 1/16 FILLS

3 NOTE 1/16 FILLS

2 NOTE 1/16 FILLS

1 NOTE 1/16 FILLS

4 2 4 2 COMBO

1 3 1 3 COMBO

LAWRENCE SCHOOL OF DRUMMING©

121

1/8 note and 1/16 Fill Combinations

A

1/8 note and 1/16 Fill Combinations

A

Easy does not equal fast!

Rhythmic Fills

1/8 and 1/16 NOTE RHYTHMIC COMBINATION FILLS

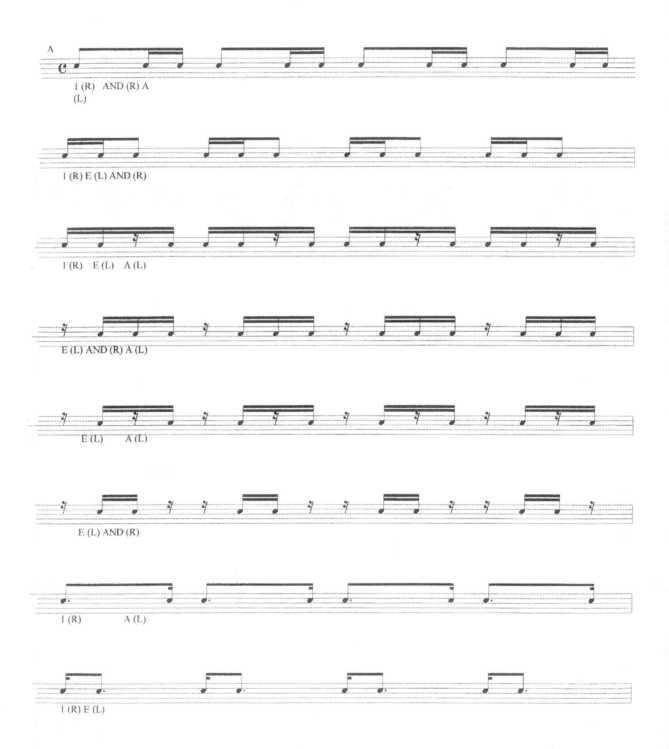

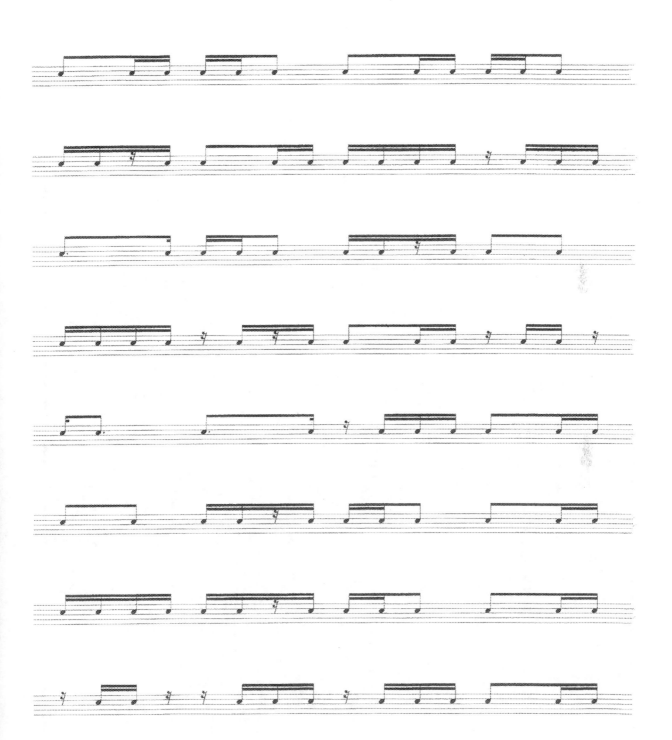

There is nothing sexy about being an idiot!

Paradiddle Fills

PARADIDDLES

Play this whole line on one drum!

Play one Paradiddle on one drum, and the other on a different one!

Play each group of four notes (half of a Paradiddle) on a different drum!

Put your two hands on two different drums, and play the whole line across!

Play the first Paradiddle on two different drums, and then move one or both hands to different drum for the second!

While leaving one hand on one drum, move the other hand to four different drums!

Move your hands any and everywhere, typically by two notes at a time!

Great Drummers have the ability to
play with controlled rage!

Ghost Stroke Fills

GHOST STROKE FILLS

SNARE VERSION

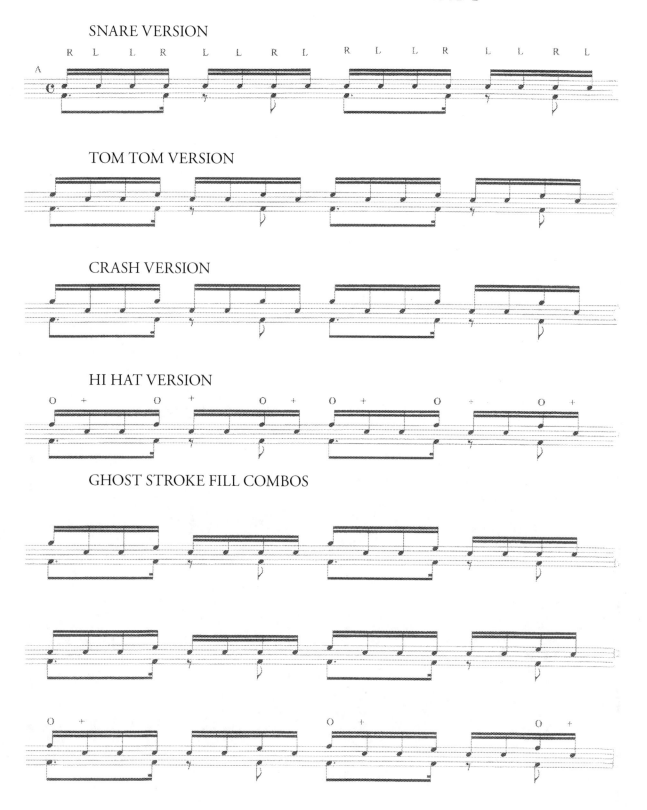

TOM TOM VERSION

CRASH VERSION

HI HAT VERSION

GHOST STROKE FILL COMBOS

Always maximize your contrast of sound!

Accent Fills

Accent fills

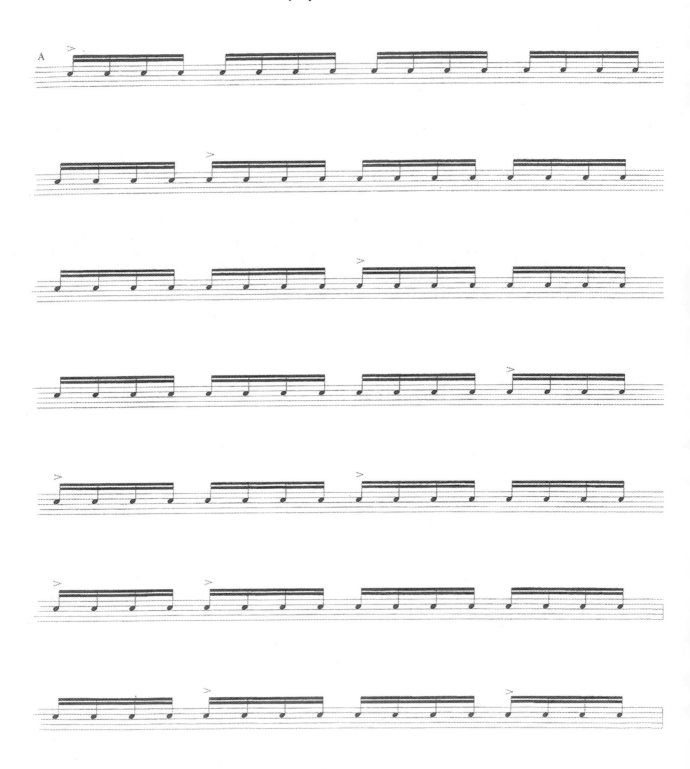

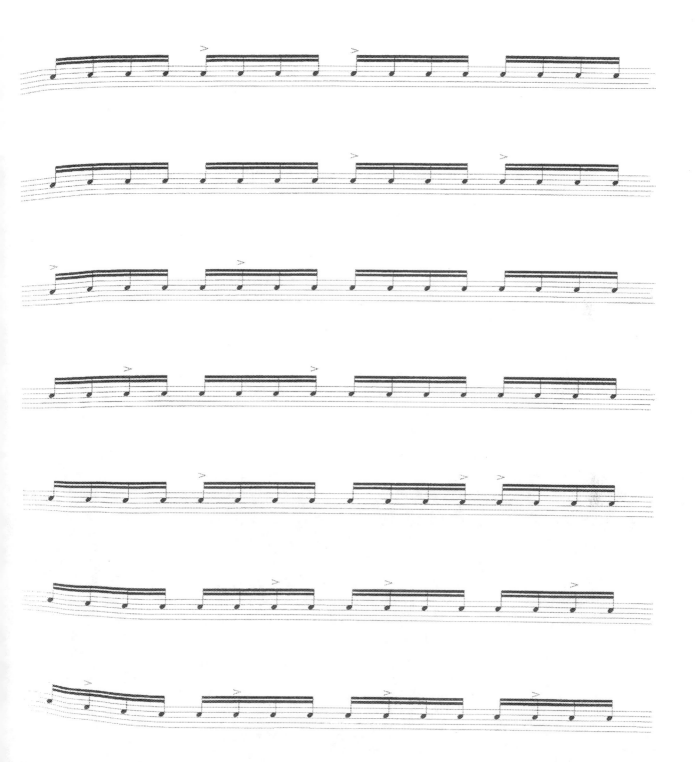

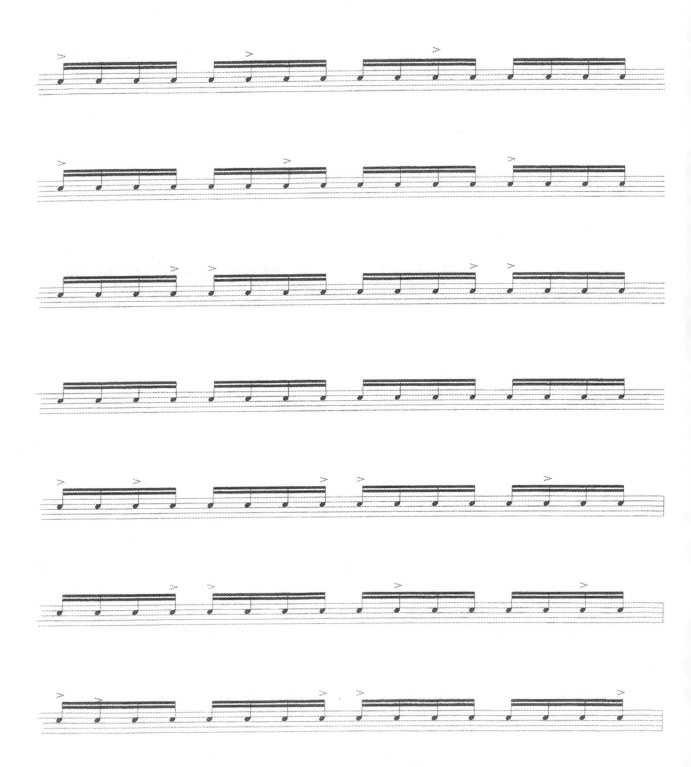

3 Characteristics of a Great Drummer:

1. Smart
2. Tough
3. Patient

Lesson Schedule

Lesson 1
- Lawrence's Golden Rule
- 4 rules of Lawrence
- 1/8 note beats p 1-4

Lesson 2
- 1/8 note beats p 5-10
- Crash Back In
- Crash sheets 1 & 2

Lesson 3
- 1/8 note beats p 11-15
- Crash Book-Cont.
- 1/8 to 1/16 Fills (4's)

Lesson 4
- Syncopated beats p 1-3
- "1 E" Exercises
- 1/8, 1/16 note fills combos

Lesson 5
- Syncopated beats p 4-6
- 1 2 3 4 Fills

Lesson 6
- Syncopated beats p 7-10
- 1 2 3 4 fills cont.

Lesson 7
- Syncopated beats p 11-13
- 1 2 3 4 combos

Lesson 8
- Syncopated beats p 14-16
- 1 2 3 4-One number beats

Lesson 9
- Paradiddle part 1
- Syncopated beats p 17-20

Lesson 10
- Paradiddle part 1-cont.
- Syncopated beats p 21-24

Lesson 11
- Paradiddle part 2
- Syncopation p 25-30

Lesson 12
- Paradiddle part 2 cont.
- Disco Rock Beats p 1-3

Lesson 13
- Rhythmic Fills
- Disco Rock beats p 4-6

Lesson 14
- Rhythmic Fills part 1 cont.
- Disco Rock beats p 7-10

Lesson 15
- Rhythmic Fills part 2
- Disco Rock beats p 11-15

Lesson 16
- Rhythmic Fills part 2 cont.
- Disco Rock beats p 16-20

Lesson 17
- Ghost Stroke Fills part 1
- Disco Rock beats p 21-25

Lesson 18
- Ghost Stroke Fills part 1 cont.
- Disco Rock beats p 26-30

Lesson 19
- Ghost Stroke Fills part 2
- 1/16 One Hand beats p 1-3

Lesson 20
- Ghost Stroke Fills part 2 cont.
- 1/16 One Hand beats p 4-6

W.I.P

<u>W</u>ORK IN <u>P</u>ROGRESS